50 Premium Wedding Food Recipes for Home

By: Kelly Johnson

Table of Contents

- Lobster Thermidor
- Truffle Risotto
- Beef Wellington
- Foie Gras Terrine
- Duck Confit
- Caviar Blini
- Oysters Rockefeller
- Seafood Paella
- Rack of Lamb with Mint Sauce
- Stuffed Quail
- Crab Cakes with Remoulade
- Filet Mignon with Bearnaise Sauce
- Lobster Bisque
- Veal Saltimbocca
- Shrimp Scampi
- Escargots Bourguignon
- Coquilles Saint-Jacques
- Chicken Cordon Bleu
- Truffled Macaroni and Cheese
- Grilled Swordfish with Lemon Butter
- Seared Scallops with Saffron Sauce
- Braised Short Ribs
- Tuna Tartare
- Caprese Salad with Burrata
- Peking Duck with Pancakes
- Stuffed Lobster Tails
- Sushi and Sashimi Platter
- Pate en Croute
- Beef Carpaccio
- Chicken Satay with Peanut Sauce
- Smoked Salmon Canapes
- Vegetarian Spring Rolls
- Roasted Vegetable Terrine
- Wild Mushroom Risotto
- Greek Mezze Platter

- Venison Medallions with Red Wine Sauce
- Sea Bass en Papillote
- Baked Alaska
- Chocolate Fondue Fountain
- Macarons Assortment
- Miniature Cheesecakes
- Raspberry White Chocolate Mousse
- Strawberry Shortcake
- Tiramisu
- Lemon Sorbet
- Gourmet Cupcakes
- Profiteroles with Vanilla Cream
- Crepes Suzette
- Chocolate Truffles
- Fruit Tartlets

Lobster Thermidor

Ingredients:

- 2 whole lobsters (about 1 1/2 pounds each), cooked and meat removed
- 4 tablespoons unsalted butter
- 1 shallot, finely chopped
- 2 tablespoons all-purpose flour
- 1/2 cup dry white wine
- 1 cup heavy cream
- 1/2 cup grated Gruyère cheese
- 2 tablespoons Dijon mustard
- 2 tablespoons chopped fresh parsley
- Salt and freshly ground black pepper, to taste
- Pinch of cayenne pepper (optional)
- Lemon wedges, for serving
- Fresh parsley sprigs, for garnish

Instructions:

1. Prepare the Lobster:
    - Preheat your oven to 400°F (200°C).
    - Cook the whole lobsters in boiling water for about 8-10 minutes until they turn bright red. Remove from water and let them cool.
    - Once cooled, remove the lobster meat from the shells. Cut the lobster meat into bite-sized chunks and set aside.
2. Make the Sauce:
    - In a large skillet or saucepan, melt 2 tablespoons of butter over medium heat. Add the chopped shallot and cook until softened, about 3-4 minutes.
    - Sprinkle the flour over the shallots and cook, stirring constantly, for 1-2 minutes to make a roux.
    - Gradually whisk in the white wine and heavy cream. Bring the mixture to a simmer, stirring constantly, until it thickens enough to coat the back of a spoon.
    - Remove the pan from the heat and stir in the grated Gruyère cheese until melted and smooth. Stir in the Dijon mustard, chopped parsley, salt, black pepper, and cayenne pepper (if using).
3. Assemble and Bake:
    - Add the cooked lobster meat to the sauce, stirring gently to combine and coat the lobster evenly.
    - Divide the lobster mixture evenly among the lobster shells or individual ovenproof dishes.
    - Melt the remaining 2 tablespoons of butter and drizzle over the lobster mixture.
    - Place the filled shells or dishes on a baking sheet and bake in the preheated oven for 10-12 minutes, or until the tops are golden brown and bubbly.

4. Serve:
    - Remove from the oven and let cool for a few minutes.
    - Garnish with fresh parsley sprigs and serve immediately, with lemon wedges on the side.

Lobster Thermidor is a decadent and luxurious dish that makes an impressive main course for a special occasion like a wedding dinner. Enjoy the creamy sauce and tender lobster meat, complemented by the flavors of Dijon mustard and Gruyère cheese.

Truffle Risotto

Ingredients:

- 1 cup Arborio rice
- 4 cups chicken or vegetable broth
- 1/2 cup dry white wine
- 1 shallot, finely chopped
- 2 cloves garlic, minced
- 2 tablespoons unsalted butter
- 1 tablespoon olive oil
- 1/4 cup grated Parmesan cheese, plus extra for serving
- 1-2 teaspoons truffle oil (adjust to taste)
- Salt and freshly ground black pepper, to taste
- Fresh chives or parsley, chopped, for garnish (optional)

Instructions:

1. Prepare the Broth:
    - In a saucepan, heat the chicken or vegetable broth over medium heat until warm. Reduce the heat to low and keep the broth warm throughout the cooking process.
2. Sauté the Aromatics:
    - In a large, deep skillet or Dutch oven, heat the olive oil and 1 tablespoon of butter over medium heat.
    - Add the chopped shallot and minced garlic. Sauté for 2-3 minutes until the shallot becomes translucent and fragrant.
3. Toast the Rice:
    - Add the Arborio rice to the skillet with the shallots and garlic. Stir to coat the rice with the oil and butter. Toast the rice for about 2 minutes, stirring frequently, until it becomes slightly translucent around the edges.
4. Deglaze with Wine:
    - Pour in the dry white wine and stir continuously until the wine is absorbed by the rice.
5. Cook the Risotto:
    - Begin adding the warm broth to the rice, one ladleful at a time. Stir frequently and allow each addition of broth to be absorbed before adding more. Adjust the heat to maintain a gentle simmer.
    - Continue adding broth and stirring for about 18-20 minutes, or until the rice is creamy and cooked al dente (tender but still firm to the bite).
6. Finish the Risotto:
    - Stir in the remaining tablespoon of butter and grated Parmesan cheese until melted and incorporated into the risotto.

- Drizzle in the truffle oil, starting with 1 teaspoon and adjusting to taste. Truffle oil is potent, so a little goes a long way.
- Season with salt and freshly ground black pepper to taste.

7. Serve:
    - Divide the truffle risotto among serving plates or bowls.
    - Garnish with additional grated Parmesan cheese and chopped fresh chives or parsley, if desired.
    - Serve immediately while hot, as risotto tends to thicken upon standing.

Truffle risotto is best enjoyed as a main course or as a side dish to complement a special meal. Its creamy texture and delicate truffle aroma make it a perfect dish for impressing guests at a wedding or any elegant gathering.

Beef Wellington

Ingredients:

- 1 whole beef tenderloin (about 2 pounds), trimmed
- Salt and freshly ground black pepper, to taste
- 2 tablespoons olive oil
- 1 tablespoon Dijon mustard
- 8 ounces mushrooms, finely chopped (button mushrooms or cremini)
- 2 cloves garlic, minced
- 1 tablespoon fresh thyme leaves, chopped
- 2 tablespoons butter
- 1/4 cup dry white wine (optional)
- 1 sheet puff pastry, thawed if frozen
- 1 egg, beaten (for egg wash)
- Salt and freshly ground black pepper, to taste

Instructions:

1. Prepare the Beef:
   - Preheat your oven to 400°F (200°C).
   - Season the beef tenderloin generously with salt and pepper.
2. Sear the Beef:
   - Heat olive oil in a large skillet over high heat. Sear the beef tenderloin on all sides until well browned, about 2-3 minutes per side. Remove from heat and let cool slightly.
   - Brush the seared beef tenderloin evenly with Dijon mustard. This adds flavor and helps the mushroom duxelles stick.
3. Make the Mushroom Duxelles:
   - In the same skillet, melt the butter over medium heat. Add the finely chopped mushrooms, minced garlic, and fresh thyme. Cook, stirring occasionally, until the mushrooms release their liquid and it evaporates, and the mushrooms are golden brown.
   - If using, pour in the white wine to deglaze the skillet, scraping up any browned bits from the bottom. Cook until the wine has evaporated. Season with salt and pepper to taste. Let cool slightly.
4. Assemble the Wellington:
   - Roll out the puff pastry on a lightly floured surface to about 1/4 inch thickness. The size should be large enough to wrap around the beef tenderloin.
   - Spread the mushroom duxelles evenly over the puff pastry, leaving a border around the edges.
   - Place the seared beef tenderloin in the center of the pastry on top of the mushroom mixture.
5. Wrap and Seal:

- Carefully fold the puff pastry over the beef tenderloin, pressing gently to seal the edges. Trim any excess pastry if necessary.
- Brush the entire pastry with beaten egg, which helps achieve a golden brown crust when baked.

6. **Bake:**
   - Place the assembled Beef Wellington on a baking sheet lined with parchment paper.
   - Bake in the preheated oven for 35-40 minutes, or until the puff pastry is golden brown and the beef reaches your desired doneness (medium-rare is recommended for tenderloin).

7. **Rest and Serve:**
   - Remove the Beef Wellington from the oven and let it rest for 10 minutes before slicing.
   - Slice into thick portions and serve hot, garnished with fresh herbs if desired.

Beef Wellington is a show-stopping dish that impresses with its layers of flavors and textures. Serve it alongside roasted vegetables or a simple green salad for a complete meal fit for a special occasion like a wedding. Enjoy the tender beef encased in crisp, golden puff pastry!

Foie Gras Terrine

Ingredients:

- 1 pound fresh foie gras (duck or goose liver), cleaned and deveined
- 1 teaspoon salt
- 1/2 teaspoon freshly ground black pepper
- 1/4 teaspoon ground nutmeg
- 1/4 cup brandy or cognac
- 1/4 cup port wine
- 1/4 cup heavy cream
- Thinly sliced truffles or truffle oil (optional, for extra flavor)

Instructions:

1. Prepare the Foie Gras:
   - Ensure the foie gras is cleaned and deveined. If necessary, remove any veins or impurities with a sharp knife.
   - Season the foie gras generously with salt, black pepper, and ground nutmeg. Sprinkle evenly over both sides.
2. Marinate the Foie Gras:
   - In a shallow dish or container, pour the brandy or cognac and port wine over the seasoned foie gras. Allow it to marinate in the refrigerator for at least 2 hours or overnight. This step enhances the flavor and texture of the foie gras.
3. Preheat the Oven:
   - Preheat your oven to 250°F (120°C).
4. Prepare the Terrine Mold:
   - Line a terrine mold or loaf pan with plastic wrap, leaving enough overhang to cover the top of the terrine later.
5. Assemble the Foie Gras Terrine:
   - Remove the foie gras from the marinade and pat dry with paper towels.
   - Arrange the foie gras pieces in the terrine mold, pressing down gently to pack them together.
   - Pour any remaining marinade and juices over the foie gras.
   - If using, layer thinly sliced truffles or drizzle truffle oil over the foie gras for extra flavor (optional).
6. Bake the Terrine:
   - Place the terrine mold in a larger baking dish. Pour hot water into the baking dish, about halfway up the sides of the terrine mold, to create a water bath.
   - Cover the terrine mold with aluminum foil.
7. Cooking the Terrine:
   - Bake in the preheated oven for 1 hour.
8. Chill and Serve:
   - Remove the terrine from the oven and let it cool to room temperature.

- Once cooled, transfer the terrine to the refrigerator and chill for at least 4 hours or overnight to allow it to set.
- To serve, carefully unmold the foie gras terrine by lifting the plastic wrap. Slice with a sharp knife and serve chilled with toasted brioche or crusty bread.

Foie gras terrine is a gourmet delicacy that showcases the rich, buttery flavor of foie gras. It's best enjoyed as an appetizer, served with a sweet wine or fruit compote to complement its richness. This simplified version retains the essence of this classic dish, making it perfect for special occasions like weddings or elegant gatherings.

Duck Confit

Ingredients:

- 4 duck legs (about 2 pounds total), preferably with thighs attached
- Salt and freshly ground black pepper
- 4 cloves garlic, peeled and smashed
- 4 sprigs fresh thyme (or 1 tablespoon dried thyme)
- 2 bay leaves
- 1/2 teaspoon black peppercorns
- 2 cups duck fat (or substitute with chicken fat or a mixture of olive oil and butter)

Instructions:

1. Preparation:
    - Pat the duck legs dry with paper towels. Season generously with salt and freshly ground black pepper on both sides.
2. Marinate:
    - Place the duck legs in a large bowl or dish. Add the smashed garlic cloves, thyme sprigs (or dried thyme), bay leaves, and black peppercorns. Toss to coat the duck legs evenly with the seasonings.
    - Cover the bowl or dish with plastic wrap and refrigerate for at least 12 hours or overnight to allow the flavors to meld.
3. Cooking:
    - Preheat your oven to 225°F (110°C).
    - Remove the duck legs from the marinade and wipe off any excess herbs and garlic. Reserve the garlic and herbs for later use.
4. Confit:
    - In a deep ovenproof skillet or Dutch oven, heat the duck fat over low heat until melted and just warm.
    - Add the duck legs, skin side down, in a single layer. The duck should be submerged in the fat. If needed, add more fat or use a smaller pan.
    - Add the reserved garlic cloves, thyme sprigs, bay leaves, and peppercorns to the fat.
5. Slow Cook:
    - Transfer the skillet or Dutch oven to the preheated oven. Cook uncovered for 2.5 to 3 hours, or until the duck is very tender and easily pulls away from the bone.
6. Cooling and Storage:
    - Remove the duck legs from the fat and transfer to a plate lined with paper towels to drain briefly.
    - Once cool enough to handle, transfer the duck legs to an airtight container or glass jar. Strain the fat through a fine-mesh sieve and pour enough strained fat over the duck legs to completely submerge them.

- - Let the duck confit cool to room temperature, then cover and refrigerate for up to several weeks. The flavors will continue to develop over time.
7. Serve:
    - To serve, gently reheat the duck confit in a skillet over medium heat until heated through and the skin is crisp.
    - Serve the duck confit hot, alongside roasted potatoes, green beans, or a salad.

Duck confit is a delicious and tender dish that showcases the rich flavor of duck cooked slowly in its own fat. It's a perfect choice for a special occasion meal, pairing well with robust red wines and rustic bread. Enjoy the tender meat and crispy skin of this classic French delicacy!

Caviar Blini

Ingredients:

For the Blini:

- 1 cup all-purpose flour
- 1 teaspoon baking powder
- 1/2 teaspoon salt
- 1 cup milk
- 1 large egg
- 2 tablespoons unsalted butter, melted
- Additional butter or oil for cooking

For Serving:

- Caviar (preferably Russian or Iranian sturgeon caviar)
- Sour cream or crème fraîche
- Fresh dill or chives, finely chopped
- Lemon wedges

Instructions:

1. Prepare the Blini Batter:
   - In a mixing bowl, whisk together the flour, baking powder, and salt.
   - In another bowl, whisk together the milk, egg, and melted butter until well combined.
   - Gradually add the wet ingredients to the dry ingredients, whisking until you have a smooth batter without lumps. Let the batter rest for about 15 minutes.
2. Cook the Blini:
   - Heat a non-stick skillet or griddle over medium heat. Lightly grease the skillet with butter or oil.
   - Pour a small amount of batter (about 2 tablespoons) onto the skillet to form small pancakes, approximately 2-3 inches in diameter.
   - Cook the blini for about 1-2 minutes on each side, or until bubbles form on the surface and the edges are set. Flip and cook for another minute until golden brown.
   - Transfer the cooked blini to a plate and cover with a clean kitchen towel to keep warm. Repeat with the remaining batter, greasing the skillet as needed.
3. Assemble the Caviar Blini:
   - To serve, place a dollop of sour cream or crème fraîche on each blini.
   - Top with a small spoonful of caviar, spreading it gently over the sour cream.
   - Garnish with finely chopped fresh dill or chives.
4. Serve:
   - Arrange the caviar blini on a serving platter.

- Serve immediately, accompanied by lemon wedges on the side for squeezing over the caviar.

Caviar blini is best enjoyed as an elegant appetizer for special occasions, such as weddings or festive gatherings. The delicate blini provide a perfect base for the rich and briny caviar, enhanced by the creamy texture of sour cream or crème fraîche and the freshness of herbs. Serve with chilled champagne or a crisp white wine to complement the flavors.

Oysters Rockefeller

Ingredients:

- 12 fresh oysters, shucked, with shells reserved
- 1/2 cup unsalted butter
- 1/2 cup breadcrumbs (preferably Panko or fresh breadcrumbs)
- 1/4 cup finely chopped parsley
- 1/4 cup finely chopped spinach (fresh or frozen, thawed and drained)
- 1/4 cup finely chopped green onions or shallots
- 2 tablespoons Pernod or other anise-flavored liqueur (optional)
- 1/4 teaspoon salt
- 1/4 teaspoon freshly ground black pepper
- 1/4 teaspoon ground nutmeg
- 1/4 cup grated Parmesan cheese
- Rock salt or coarse salt, for serving

Instructions:

1. Prepare the Oysters:
    - Preheat your oven to 450°F (230°C).
    - Shuck the oysters, reserving the bottom (deeper) half of the shell and discarding the top shell. Clean the shells thoroughly and arrange them on a baking sheet lined with rock salt or coarse salt to stabilize them.
2. Make the Rockefeller Sauce:
    - In a saucepan, melt the butter over medium heat. Add the breadcrumbs and cook, stirring constantly, until lightly toasted and golden brown.
    - Add the chopped parsley, spinach, green onions (or shallots), and cook for another 2-3 minutes until the vegetables are tender.
    - Stir in the Pernod (if using), salt, black pepper, and nutmeg. Cook for another minute, then remove from heat.
3. Assemble and Bake:
    - Spoon a small amount of the Rockefeller sauce over each oyster in its shell, covering the oyster completely.
    - Sprinkle grated Parmesan cheese evenly over the top of each oyster.
4. Bake or Broil:
    - Bake the Oysters Rockefeller in the preheated oven for 10-12 minutes, or until the sauce is bubbling and the edges are lightly browned.
    - Alternatively, you can broil the oysters on high for 5-7 minutes, watching carefully to avoid burning.
5. Serve:
    - Remove the Oysters Rockefeller from the oven and let them cool slightly.
    - Arrange the baked oysters on a serving platter lined with rock salt or coarse salt to stabilize them.

- Serve immediately as an elegant appetizer, garnished with lemon wedges if desired.

Oysters Rockefeller is a decadent and flavorful dish that showcases the briny sweetness of fresh oysters combined with a rich, herbaceous sauce. It's perfect for special occasions and pairs well with a chilled glass of white wine or Champagne. Enjoy the luxurious flavors of this classic seafood dish!

Seafood Paella

Ingredients:

- 1 cup Arborio rice (or Spanish short-grain rice, such as Bomba rice)
- 4 cups seafood or chicken broth
- 1/2 teaspoon saffron threads (optional, for color and flavor)
- 1/4 cup olive oil
- 1 onion, finely chopped
- 4 cloves garlic, minced
- 1 red bell pepper, diced
- 1 tomato, diced
- 1 teaspoon smoked paprika
- 1 teaspoon dried oregano
- Salt and freshly ground black pepper, to taste
- 1/2 pound shrimp, peeled and deveined
- 1/2 pound mussels, cleaned and debearded
- 1/2 pound squid rings
- 1/2 cup frozen peas (optional)
- Lemon wedges, for serving
- Fresh parsley, chopped, for garnish

Instructions:

1. Prepare the Saffron Broth:
    - In a small saucepan, heat the seafood or chicken broth over medium heat until warm. If using saffron threads, add them to the warm broth to infuse their flavor and color. Keep the broth warm throughout the cooking process.
2. Sauté the Aromatics:
    - In a large, shallow skillet or paella pan, heat the olive oil over medium heat. Add the chopped onion and sauté until softened, about 3-4 minutes.
    - Stir in the minced garlic and diced red bell pepper. Cook for another 2-3 minutes until the peppers begin to soften.
3. Add Tomatoes and Seasonings:
    - Add the diced tomato, smoked paprika, and dried oregano to the skillet. Cook, stirring occasionally, for about 5 minutes until the tomatoes break down and the mixture becomes fragrant.
    - Season with salt and freshly ground black pepper to taste.
4. Cook the Rice:
    - Stir in the Arborio rice (or Spanish rice) until evenly coated with the tomato mixture.
    - Pour in the warm saffron-infused broth, stirring gently to combine. Bring to a simmer and cook uncovered over medium-low heat for about 15-20 minutes, or until the rice is almost tender and most of the liquid is absorbed.

5. Add Seafood and Peas:
   - Arrange the shrimp, mussels, and squid rings on top of the rice mixture. Scatter the frozen peas (if using) evenly over the seafood.
6. Simmer and Finish:
   - Cover the skillet or paella pan with a lid or foil and cook for another 8-10 minutes, or until the seafood is cooked through and the rice is tender. The mussels should open, and the shrimp should turn pink.
7. Serve:
   - Remove from heat and let the paella rest, covered, for a few minutes.
   - Garnish with chopped fresh parsley and serve hot, accompanied by lemon wedges for squeezing over the paella.

Seafood paella is a festive and impressive dish that's perfect for special occasions like weddings. The combination of seafood, flavorful rice, and aromatic saffron creates a dish that is both satisfying and full of Mediterranean flair. Enjoy this delicious Spanish classic with family and friends!

Rack of Lamb with Mint Sauce

Ingredients:

For the Rack of Lamb:

- 1 rack of lamb (about 1.5 - 2 pounds), trimmed and frenched (about 8 ribs)
- Salt and freshly ground black pepper
- 2 tablespoons olive oil
- 2 cloves garlic, minced
- 2 teaspoons fresh rosemary, chopped (or 1 teaspoon dried rosemary)
- 1 teaspoon fresh thyme leaves (or 1/2 teaspoon dried thyme)

For the Mint Sauce:

- 1/2 cup fresh mint leaves, finely chopped
- 1/4 cup red wine vinegar
- 2 tablespoons sugar
- 2 tablespoons water
- Salt and freshly ground black pepper, to taste

Instructions:

1. Prepare the Rack of Lamb:
    - Preheat your oven to 400°F (200°C).
    - Season the rack of lamb generously with salt and freshly ground black pepper on all sides.
2. Sear the Lamb:
    - Heat olive oil in a large ovenproof skillet over medium-high heat.
    - Add the rack of lamb, fat side down, and sear for 3-4 minutes until golden brown. Turn and sear the other side for another 3-4 minutes.
3. Add Flavorings:
    - Reduce the heat to medium. Add minced garlic, chopped rosemary, and thyme to the skillet.
    - Cook, stirring the herbs and garlic around the lamb, for about 1 minute to release their flavors.
4. Roast the Lamb:
    - Transfer the skillet to the preheated oven.
    - Roast the rack of lamb for 15-20 minutes for medium-rare, or until an instant-read thermometer inserted into the thickest part of the meat registers 125-130°F (52-54°C) for medium-rare or 135-140°F (57-60°C) for medium.
5. Rest the Lamb:
    - Remove the lamb from the oven and transfer it to a cutting board. Cover loosely with foil and let it rest for 10 minutes. This allows the juices to redistribute and the lamb to become more tender.

6. Make the Mint Sauce:
    - While the lamb is resting, prepare the mint sauce. In a small saucepan, combine chopped mint leaves, red wine vinegar, sugar, and water.
    - Bring to a simmer over medium heat, stirring until the sugar dissolves. Simmer gently for about 2-3 minutes.
    - Season with salt and freshly ground black pepper to taste. Remove from heat and let cool slightly.
7. Slice and Serve:
    - Slice the rack of lamb between the bones into individual chops.
    - Arrange the lamb chops on a serving platter and drizzle with the mint sauce.
    - Serve immediately, accompanied by roasted potatoes, steamed vegetables, or your favorite side dishes.

Rack of lamb with mint sauce is a sophisticated dish that's perfect for special occasions like weddings. The tender, juicy lamb pairs beautifully with the bright, herbaceous mint sauce, creating a delightful combination of flavors. Enjoy this elegant dish with your guests and celebrate in style!

Stuffed Quail

Ingredients:

For the Quail:

- 4 whole quails, cleaned and patted dry
- Salt and freshly ground black pepper
- 2 tablespoons olive oil

For the Stuffing:

- 1/2 cup breadcrumbs (preferably Panko or fresh breadcrumbs)
- 2 tablespoons unsalted butter
- 1 small onion, finely chopped
- 2 cloves garlic, minced
- 1/4 cup chopped fresh herbs (such as parsley, thyme, and rosemary)
- 1/4 cup chopped dried fruits (such as cranberries or apricots)
- 1/4 cup chopped nuts (such as walnuts or pecans)
- Salt and freshly ground black pepper, to taste

For the Glaze:

- 1/4 cup balsamic vinegar
- 2 tablespoons honey
- 1 tablespoon Dijon mustard

Instructions:

1. Prepare the Stuffing:
   - In a skillet, melt the butter over medium heat. Add the chopped onion and garlic, and sauté until softened, about 3-4 minutes.
   - Stir in the breadcrumbs, chopped herbs, dried fruits, and nuts. Cook for another 2-3 minutes until the breadcrumbs are lightly toasted and the mixture is well combined.
   - Season with salt and freshly ground black pepper to taste. Remove from heat and let cool slightly.
2. Prepare the Quail:
   - Preheat your oven to 400°F (200°C).
   - Season the quails inside and out with salt and freshly ground black pepper.
   - Stuff each quail cavity with the prepared stuffing mixture, pressing gently to pack it in.
3. Truss the Quail:
   - Use kitchen twine to truss the quail legs together and secure the wings close to the body. This helps the quail cook evenly and keeps the stuffing in place.

4. Sear the Quail:
   - Heat olive oil in an ovenproof skillet over medium-high heat.
   - Add the stuffed quails to the skillet and sear on all sides until golden brown, about 2-3 minutes per side.
5. Glaze and Roast:
   - In a small bowl, whisk together the balsamic vinegar, honey, and Dijon mustard to make the glaze.
   - Brush the quails with the glaze, coating them evenly.
   - Transfer the skillet to the preheated oven and roast the quails for 15-20 minutes, or until the quails are cooked through and the internal temperature reaches 160°F (70°C).
6. Rest and Serve:
   - Remove the stuffed quails from the oven and let them rest for 5 minutes before serving.
   - To serve, carefully remove the kitchen twine from each quail.
   - Arrange the stuffed quails on serving plates and drizzle any remaining glaze over the top.
   - Serve immediately, accompanied by roasted vegetables, wild rice, or a fresh salad.

Stuffed quail is a sophisticated dish that impresses with its presentation and flavors. The tender quail meat, combined with the savory-sweet stuffing and tangy glaze, creates a harmonious blend of textures and tastes. Enjoy this elegant dish with your guests for a memorable dining experience!

Crab Cakes with Remoulade

Ingredients:

For the Crab Cakes:

- 1 pound lump crab meat, picked over for shells
- 1/2 cup Panko breadcrumbs (or other breadcrumbs)
- 1/4 cup mayonnaise
- 1 large egg
- 2 tablespoons chopped fresh parsley
- 1 tablespoon Dijon mustard
- 1 tablespoon Worcestershire sauce
- 1 teaspoon Old Bay seasoning (or to taste)
- Salt and freshly ground black pepper, to taste
- 2 tablespoons olive oil or vegetable oil, for frying

For the Remoulade Sauce:

- 1/2 cup mayonnaise
- 2 tablespoons Dijon mustard
- 1 tablespoon capers, chopped
- 1 tablespoon chopped fresh parsley
- 1 tablespoon chopped green onions (scallions)
- 1 tablespoon fresh lemon juice
- 1 teaspoon hot sauce (such as Tabasco), optional
- Salt and freshly ground black pepper, to taste

Instructions:

1. Prepare the Crab Cakes:
   - In a large bowl, gently combine the lump crab meat with the breadcrumbs, mayonnaise, egg, chopped parsley, Dijon mustard, Worcestershire sauce, Old Bay seasoning, salt, and pepper. Be careful not to break up the crab meat too much; you want to keep the chunks intact.
2. Form the Crab Cakes:
   - Divide the crab mixture into 8 equal portions. Shape each portion into a patty, about 1 inch thick. Place the formed crab cakes on a plate or baking sheet lined with parchment paper.
3. Cook the Crab Cakes:
   - In a large skillet, heat olive oil or vegetable oil over medium heat.
   - Carefully place the crab cakes in the skillet and cook until golden brown and crisp, about 4-5 minutes per side. Use a spatula to gently flip the crab cakes halfway through cooking. Add more oil if necessary.
4. Make the Remoulade Sauce:

- While the crab cakes are cooking, prepare the remoulade sauce. In a small bowl, whisk together mayonnaise, Dijon mustard, chopped capers, chopped parsley, chopped green onions, lemon juice, hot sauce (if using), salt, and pepper until well combined. Adjust seasoning to taste.
5. Serve:
    - Remove the crab cakes from the skillet and transfer to a serving platter or individual plates.
    - Serve the crab cakes hot, accompanied by the remoulade sauce on the side for dipping or drizzling over the top.
    - Garnish with additional chopped parsley or lemon wedges if desired.

Crab cakes with remoulade sauce are best enjoyed immediately while they are still warm and crispy. They make a fantastic appetizer or main dish for any occasion, combining the delicate flavor of crab meat with the zesty and creamy remoulade sauce. Serve alongside a fresh green salad or crusty bread for a complete meal.

Filet Mignon with Bearnaise Sauce

Ingredients:

For the Filet Mignon:

- 4 filet mignon steaks, about 6-8 ounces each, preferably at room temperature
- Salt and freshly ground black pepper
- 2 tablespoons olive oil or vegetable oil

For the Béarnaise Sauce:

- 1/4 cup white wine vinegar or tarragon vinegar
- 1/4 cup dry white wine
- 2 tablespoons finely chopped shallots
- 2 tablespoons chopped fresh tarragon (or 2 teaspoons dried tarragon)
- 3 large egg yolks
- 1/2 cup unsalted butter, melted and warm
- Salt and freshly ground black pepper, to taste
- 1 tablespoon fresh lemon juice, optional

For Serving:

- Fresh tarragon leaves, chopped (for garnish)
- Lemon wedges (optional)

Instructions:

1. Prepare the Filet Mignon:
    - Preheat your grill or a large skillet over medium-high heat.
    - Season the filet mignon steaks generously with salt and freshly ground black pepper on both sides.
2. Cook the Filet Mignon:
    - Drizzle olive oil or vegetable oil over the steaks and rub to coat evenly.
    - Place the steaks on the preheated grill or skillet. Cook the filet mignon for about 4-5 minutes per side for medium-rare, or adjust cooking time to your desired doneness (5-6 minutes for medium, 7-8 minutes for well-done).
    - Use tongs to flip the steaks only once during cooking to ensure a good sear. Let the steaks rest for a few minutes before serving.
3. Make the Béarnaise Sauce:
    - In a small saucepan, combine white wine vinegar (or tarragon vinegar), white wine, chopped shallots, and chopped fresh tarragon (or dried tarragon). Bring to a boil over medium-high heat, then reduce the heat and simmer until the mixture is reduced by half. Remove from heat and let cool slightly.
    - In a heatproof bowl, whisk the egg yolks until smooth.

- Gradually whisk the warm melted butter into the egg yolks, a few tablespoons at a time, until the sauce thickens and becomes smooth.
- Slowly whisk in the reduced vinegar-wine mixture into the egg yolk mixture, continuing to whisk until well combined. Season with salt and freshly ground black pepper to taste. If desired, add fresh lemon juice for extra tanginess.

4. Serve:
    - Arrange the cooked filet mignon steaks on serving plates.
    - Spoon the Béarnaise sauce generously over each steak.
    - Garnish with chopped fresh tarragon leaves and serve immediately, accompanied by lemon wedges on the side if desired.

Filet mignon with Béarnaise sauce is a luxurious dish that's perfect for special occasions. The tender, juicy steak pairs beautifully with the creamy and flavorful Béarnaise sauce, creating a restaurant-quality meal at home. Serve with roasted vegetables, mashed potatoes, or a fresh green salad for a complete and elegant dining experience. Enjoy!

Lobster Bisque

Ingredients:

- 2 lobsters (about 1.5 - 2 pounds each), cooked and meat removed
- 4 tablespoons unsalted butter
- 1 onion, chopped
- 2 carrots, chopped
- 2 celery stalks, chopped
- 2 cloves garlic, minced
- 2 tablespoons tomato paste
- 1/4 cup brandy or cognac (optional)
- 4 cups seafood stock or fish stock
- 1 cup dry white wine
- 2 cups heavy cream
- 1 bay leaf
- 1 teaspoon fresh thyme leaves (or 1/2 teaspoon dried thyme)
- Salt and freshly ground black pepper, to taste
- Cayenne pepper, to taste (optional)
- Chopped fresh chives, for garnish

Instructions:

1. Prepare the Lobster Stock:
    - Remove the meat from the cooked lobsters and set aside for later. Reserve the shells and any juices.
    - In a large pot, melt 2 tablespoons of butter over medium heat. Add the lobster shells and cook, stirring occasionally, until they turn bright red and release their juices, about 5-7 minutes.
    - Add chopped onion, carrots, celery, and garlic to the pot. Cook, stirring occasionally, until the vegetables are softened, about 5 minutes.
    - Stir in tomato paste and cook for another 2 minutes.
    - If using, add brandy or cognac to the pot and cook for 1-2 minutes, scraping any browned bits from the bottom of the pot.
    - Pour in seafood stock and white wine. Bring to a simmer, then reduce heat to low. Add bay leaf and thyme. Simmer gently, uncovered, for about 30 minutes to allow the flavors to meld.
2. Blend and Strain:
    - Remove the pot from heat and let it cool slightly. Remove and discard the bay leaf.
    - Use an immersion blender or transfer the mixture to a blender (in batches if necessary) and blend until smooth.
    - Strain the blended mixture through a fine-mesh sieve or cheesecloth into a clean pot, pressing down on solids to extract as much liquid as possible. Discard solids.

3. Finish the Bisque:
   - Return the strained liquid to the stove over medium heat. Stir in heavy cream and bring to a simmer.
   - Chop the reserved lobster meat into bite-sized pieces and add it to the bisque. Cook gently for 5-7 minutes, or until the lobster meat is heated through and tender.
   - Season the bisque with salt, freshly ground black pepper, and cayenne pepper (if using), adjusting to taste.
4. Serve:
   - Ladle the hot lobster bisque into bowls.
   - Garnish each serving with chopped fresh chives.
   - Serve immediately, accompanied by crusty bread or oyster crackers.

Lobster bisque is a decadent and flavorful soup that makes an impressive starter for a special meal. The rich, creamy texture and delicate seafood flavor make it a favorite among seafood lovers. Enjoy this homemade lobster bisque with loved ones for a restaurant-worthy dining experience at home.

Veal Saltimbocca

Ingredients:

- 4 veal cutlets (about 4-6 ounces each), pounded to about 1/4-inch thickness
- Salt and freshly ground black pepper
- 8 thin slices prosciutto
- 8 fresh sage leaves
- All-purpose flour, for dredging
- 4 tablespoons unsalted butter
- 1/2 cup dry white wine
- 1/2 cup chicken or veal broth
- 1 tablespoon fresh lemon juice
- 1 tablespoon capers, drained (optional)
- Chopped fresh parsley, for garnish

Instructions:

1. Prepare the Veal Cutlets:
    - Season both sides of each veal cutlet with salt and freshly ground black pepper.
    - Place 2 slices of prosciutto on each veal cutlet, covering them completely.
    - Place 2 sage leaves on top of the prosciutto on each cutlet, pressing them lightly to adhere.
2. Dredge and Cook the Veal:
    - Dredge each veal cutlet in flour, shaking off any excess.
    - In a large skillet, heat 2 tablespoons of butter over medium-high heat until melted and foamy.
    - Add the veal cutlets to the skillet, prosciutto-side down. Cook for 2-3 minutes until the prosciutto is crisp and lightly browned.
    - Flip the cutlets and cook on the other side for another 2-3 minutes until the veal is cooked through and golden brown. Transfer the cooked cutlets to a plate and tent with foil to keep warm.
3. Make the Sauce:
    - Deglaze the skillet with white wine, scraping up any browned bits from the bottom of the pan.
    - Add chicken or veal broth, lemon juice, and capers (if using). Bring the sauce to a simmer and cook for 3-4 minutes until slightly reduced.
    - Stir in the remaining 2 tablespoons of butter until melted and the sauce is smooth. Season with salt and pepper to taste.
4. Serve:
    - Arrange the veal saltimbocca on serving plates.
    - Spoon the sauce over the veal cutlets.
    - Garnish with chopped fresh parsley.
    - Serve immediately, accompanied by your favorite side dishes such as sautéed spinach, risotto, or roasted potatoes.

Veal Saltimbocca is a delicious and elegant dish that showcases the delicate flavors of veal, salty prosciutto, and aromatic sage. Enjoy this classic Italian favorite for a special dinner at home, paired with a glass of white wine for a complete dining experience.

Shrimp Scampi

Ingredients:

- 1 pound large shrimp, peeled and deveined
- Salt and freshly ground black pepper, to taste
- 4 tablespoons unsalted butter
- 4 tablespoons olive oil
- 4 cloves garlic, minced
- 1/2 cup white wine (such as Sauvignon Blanc or Pinot Grigio)
- 1/4 teaspoon red pepper flakes (optional)
- Zest of 1 lemon
- Juice of 1 lemon
- 1/4 cup chopped fresh parsley
- Cooked pasta or crusty bread, for serving

Instructions:

1. Prepare the Shrimp:
   - Pat the shrimp dry with paper towels and season with salt and freshly ground black pepper.
2. Cook the Shrimp:
   - In a large skillet, heat 2 tablespoons of butter and 2 tablespoons of olive oil over medium-high heat until the butter is melted and bubbly.
   - Add the minced garlic and cook for about 30 seconds until fragrant, stirring constantly to prevent burning.
   - Add the seasoned shrimp to the skillet in a single layer. Cook for 1-2 minutes per side, until the shrimp turn pink and opaque. Be careful not to overcook them. Remove the shrimp from the skillet and set aside.
3. Make the Sauce:
   - In the same skillet, add the white wine and red pepper flakes (if using). Bring to a simmer and cook for 2-3 minutes, scraping up any browned bits from the bottom of the skillet.
   - Stir in the remaining 2 tablespoons of butter until melted and the sauce starts to thicken slightly.
   - Add the lemon zest and lemon juice to the sauce. Stir to combine.
4. Combine and Serve:
   - Return the cooked shrimp to the skillet, tossing gently to coat them in the sauce.
   - Sprinkle chopped fresh parsley over the shrimp scampi.
   - Serve immediately over cooked pasta or with crusty bread for dipping, garnished with additional parsley if desired.

Shrimp scampi is a flavorful and satisfying dish that comes together in minutes. The combination of garlic, butter, white wine, and lemon creates a light and tangy sauce that perfectly complements the sweet flavor of the shrimp. Enjoy this classic seafood dish as a quick and delicious meal any day of the week!

Escargots Bourguignon

Ingredients:

- 24 canned or frozen escargot shells (or use ceramic escargot dishes)
- 24 cooked snails (canned or frozen, drained and rinsed if necessary)
- 6 tablespoons unsalted butter, softened
- 2 cloves garlic, minced
- 2 tablespoons chopped fresh parsley
- Salt and freshly ground black pepper, to taste
- 1/4 cup dry white wine
- 1 French baguette, sliced and toasted (for serving)

Instructions:

1. Prepare the Escargots:
    - If using canned or frozen escargots, drain and rinse them under cold water to remove any excess liquid.
2. Prepare the Butter Mixture:
    - In a small bowl, combine softened butter, minced garlic, chopped parsley, salt, and freshly ground black pepper. Mix until well combined.
3. Assemble the Escargots:
    - Preheat your oven to 400°F (200°C).
    - Place each escargot shell (or ceramic dish) in a baking dish.
    - Put one cooked snail into each shell.
    - Spoon about 1 teaspoon of the garlic-parsley butter mixture over each snail.
4. Bake the Escargots:
    - Pour the dry white wine around the escargots in the baking dish.
    - Bake in the preheated oven for 10-12 minutes, or until the butter is bubbling and the snails are heated through.
5. Serve:
    - Remove the escargots from the oven.
    - Serve immediately, using a fork and escargot tongs (if available) to hold the shells steady while extracting the snails.
    - Accompany with toasted French baguette slices for dipping into the garlic-parsley butter.

Escargots Bourguignon is a delightful appetizer that pairs well with a crisp white wine. The buttery, garlic-infused sauce complements the tender texture and mild flavor of the snails, making it a unique and elegant dish to enjoy at home or as part of a special occasion meal. Bon appétit!

Coquilles Saint-Jacques

Ingredients:

- 1 pound sea scallops, rinsed and patted dry
- Salt and freshly ground black pepper, to taste
- 2 tablespoons unsalted butter
- 2 tablespoons olive oil
- 1 shallot, finely chopped
- 8 ounces mushrooms, sliced
- 1/2 cup dry white wine
- 1 cup heavy cream
- 1/2 cup grated Gruyère cheese (or another melting cheese like Emmental or Swiss)
- 1/4 cup breadcrumbs
- 2 tablespoons chopped fresh parsley
- Lemon wedges, for serving

Instructions:

1. **Prepare the Scallops:**
   - Pat the scallops dry with paper towels and season them with salt and pepper on both sides.
2. **Sear the Scallops:**
   - In a large skillet, heat 1 tablespoon of butter and 1 tablespoon of olive oil over medium-high heat until hot.
   - Add the scallops to the skillet in a single layer (work in batches if necessary to avoid overcrowding). Sear the scallops for about 2-3 minutes on each side, until golden brown and cooked through. Remove the scallops from the skillet and set aside.
3. **Make the Sauce:**
   - In the same skillet, add the remaining butter and olive oil if needed.
   - Add the chopped shallot and sliced mushrooms. Sauté for 5-6 minutes, until the mushrooms are softened and golden brown.
   - Pour in the dry white wine and cook for 2-3 minutes, allowing it to reduce slightly.
   - Stir in the heavy cream and bring the mixture to a simmer. Cook for another 2-3 minutes until the sauce thickens slightly.
4. **Assemble and Bake:**
   - Preheat your oven's broiler.
   - Arrange the seared scallops in individual gratin dishes or a baking dish.
   - Pour the mushroom cream sauce over the scallops, ensuring they are well coated.
   - Sprinkle the grated Gruyère cheese evenly over the top, followed by the breadcrumbs.
5. **Broil the Coquilles Saint-Jacques:**
   - Place the gratin dishes or baking dish under the broiler for 3-4 minutes, or until the cheese is melted and bubbly, and the breadcrumbs are golden brown.

          - Watch carefully to prevent burning.
    6. Serve:
          - Remove the Coquilles Saint-Jacques from the oven.
          - Garnish with chopped fresh parsley and serve immediately, accompanied by lemon wedges on the side.

Coquilles Saint-Jacques is a luxurious and flavorful dish that highlights the delicate sweetness of scallops in a rich, creamy sauce. Enjoy this classic French dish as an elegant appetizer or main course for a special occasion meal at home.

Chicken Cordon Bleu

Ingredients:

- 4 boneless, skinless chicken breasts
- Salt and freshly ground black pepper, to taste
- 4 slices Swiss cheese (or Gruyère cheese)
- 4 slices ham (thinly sliced, deli-style)
- 1/2 cup all-purpose flour
- 2 large eggs
- 1 cup breadcrumbs (preferably Panko breadcrumbs)
- 1/2 cup grated Parmesan cheese
- 1 teaspoon garlic powder
- 1 teaspoon paprika
- 2 tablespoons olive oil or vegetable oil
- Toothpicks (optional, for securing)

Instructions:

1. Prepare the Chicken:
    - Preheat your oven to 375°F (190°C).
    - Place each chicken breast between plastic wrap or parchment paper. Use a meat mallet or rolling pin to pound the chicken to an even thickness of about 1/4 inch. This makes it easier to roll and cook evenly.
2. Assemble the Chicken Cordon Bleu:
    - Season both sides of each chicken breast with salt and pepper.
    - Place a slice of Swiss cheese and a slice of ham on each chicken breast.
    - Carefully roll up each chicken breast, starting from the narrowest end, to enclose the cheese and ham inside. Secure with toothpicks if needed to hold the roll together.
3. Coat the Chicken:
    - Set up three shallow bowls or plates: one with flour, one with beaten eggs, and one with a mixture of breadcrumbs, grated Parmesan cheese, garlic powder, and paprika.
    - Roll each chicken breast first in the flour, shaking off any excess.
    - Dip the floured chicken breast into the beaten eggs, ensuring it is well coated.
    - Finally, roll the chicken breast in the breadcrumb mixture, pressing gently to adhere the breadcrumbs.
4. Cook the Chicken:
    - In a large oven-safe skillet or frying pan, heat olive oil or vegetable oil over medium-high heat.
    - Carefully place the breaded chicken breasts in the skillet, seam side down. Cook for about 3-4 minutes on each side, or until golden brown and crispy.
5. Finish in the Oven:
    - Transfer the skillet to the preheated oven.

- - Bake the chicken for 20-25 minutes, or until the internal temperature reaches 165°F (75°C) and the chicken is cooked through.
6. Serve:
    - Remove the toothpicks from the chicken before serving.
    - Slice the Chicken Cordon Bleu crosswise into rounds and serve hot.
    - Optionally, garnish with chopped fresh parsley and serve with a side of vegetables, salad, or mashed potatoes.

Chicken Cordon Bleu is a delightful dish that combines savory chicken with the richness of melted cheese and ham, all wrapped up in a crispy breadcrumb coating. It's perfect for a special dinner or when you want to impress guests with a classic French-inspired dish. Enjoy!

Truffled Macaroni and Cheese

Ingredients:

- 8 ounces elbow macaroni (or any pasta shape you prefer)
- 2 tablespoons unsalted butter
- 2 tablespoons all-purpose flour
- 2 cups whole milk (or half-and-half for a richer sauce)
- 2 cups shredded cheese (such as sharp cheddar, Gruyère, or a combination)
- Salt and freshly ground black pepper, to taste
- 1-2 tablespoons truffle oil (adjust to taste)
- 1/4 cup grated Parmesan cheese
- Optional: truffle salt or additional grated truffle for garnish

Instructions:

1. Cook the Pasta:
    - Cook the elbow macaroni according to package instructions in salted boiling water until al dente. Drain and set aside.
2. Make the Cheese Sauce:
    - In a large saucepan, melt the butter over medium heat.
    - Stir in the flour and cook for 1-2 minutes, stirring constantly, to make a roux.
    - Gradually whisk in the milk (or half-and-half) until smooth. Cook, stirring frequently, until the mixture begins to thicken, about 5-7 minutes.
    - Reduce the heat to low and stir in the shredded cheese until melted and smooth. Season with salt and pepper to taste.
3. Add Truffle Flavor:
    - Remove the cheese sauce from heat and stir in the truffle oil. Start with 1 tablespoon and taste, adding more if desired for stronger truffle flavor.
    - Stir in the cooked macaroni until evenly coated with the cheese sauce.
4. Bake (Optional):
    - Preheat your oven to 350°F (175°C).
    - Transfer the truffled macaroni and cheese to a baking dish. Sprinkle grated Parmesan cheese on top.
    - Bake for 20-25 minutes, until bubbly and golden brown on top.
5. Serve:
    - Remove from the oven and let it cool slightly before serving.
    - Optionally, garnish with a sprinkle of truffle salt or additional grated truffle for extra flavor.

Truffled macaroni and cheese is a decadent and flavorful dish that combines the creamy comfort of traditional macaroni and cheese with the earthy aroma of truffles. It's perfect as a main dish or a side dish for a special occasion. Enjoy this indulgent treat with loved ones for a memorable meal!

Grilled Swordfish with Lemon Butter

Ingredients:

- 4 swordfish steaks, about 6 ounces each
- Salt and freshly ground black pepper, to taste
- Olive oil, for brushing

For the Lemon Butter Sauce:

- 1/2 cup unsalted butter
- Zest of 1 lemon
- Juice of 1 lemon
- 2 cloves garlic, minced
- 2 tablespoons chopped fresh parsley
- Salt and freshly ground black pepper, to taste

Instructions:

1. Prepare the Swordfish:
    - Pat the swordfish steaks dry with paper towels.
    - Season both sides of the swordfish steaks with salt and freshly ground black pepper.
2. Preheat the Grill:
    - Preheat your grill to medium-high heat. Make sure the grates are clean and lightly oiled to prevent sticking.
3. Grill the Swordfish:
    - Brush both sides of the swordfish steaks with olive oil to prevent them from sticking to the grill.
    - Place the swordfish steaks on the preheated grill. Grill for about 4-5 minutes on each side, depending on the thickness of the steaks, until the fish is cooked through and has grill marks. The internal temperature should reach 145°F (63°C).
4. Make the Lemon Butter Sauce:
    - While the swordfish is grilling, prepare the lemon butter sauce. In a small saucepan, melt the butter over medium heat.
    - Add the minced garlic and cook for 1-2 minutes until fragrant, stirring frequently.
    - Stir in the lemon zest and lemon juice. Season with salt and freshly ground black pepper to taste.
    - Remove from heat and stir in the chopped fresh parsley.
5. Serve:
    - Transfer the grilled swordfish steaks to serving plates.
    - Spoon the lemon butter sauce over the swordfish steaks.
    - Garnish with additional chopped parsley or lemon slices if desired.
    - Serve immediately, accompanied by your favorite side dishes such as grilled vegetables, rice, or a fresh salad.

Grilled swordfish with lemon butter is a flavorful and satisfying dish that's perfect for a summer barbecue or any special occasion. The lemon butter sauce adds a bright, citrusy note that complements the mild, meaty flavor of the swordfish beautifully. Enjoy this simple and elegant seafood dish with family and friends!

Seared Scallops with Saffron Sauce

Ingredients:

- 2 lobsters (about 1.5 - 2 pounds each), cooked and meat removed
- 4 tablespoons unsalted butter
- 1 onion, chopped
- 2 carrots, chopped
- 2 celery stalks, chopped
- 2 cloves garlic, minced
- 2 tablespoons tomato paste
- 1/4 cup brandy or cognac (optional)
- 4 cups seafood stock or fish stock
- 1 cup dry white wine
- 2 cups heavy cream
- 1 bay leaf
- 1 teaspoon fresh thyme leaves (or 1/2 teaspoon dried thyme)
- Salt and freshly ground black pepper, to taste
- Cayenne pepper, to taste (optional)
- Chopped fresh chives, for garnish

Instructions:

1. Prepare the Lobster Stock:
   - Remove the meat from the cooked lobsters and set aside for later. Reserve the shells and any juices.
   - In a large pot, melt 2 tablespoons of butter over medium heat. Add the lobster shells and cook, stirring occasionally, until they turn bright red and release their juices, about 5-7 minutes.
   - Add chopped onion, carrots, celery, and garlic to the pot. Cook, stirring occasionally, until the vegetables are softened, about 5 minutes.
   - Stir in tomato paste and cook for another 2 minutes.
   - If using, add brandy or cognac to the pot and cook for 1-2 minutes, scraping any browned bits from the bottom of the pot.
   - Pour in seafood stock and white wine. Bring to a simmer, then reduce heat to low. Add bay leaf and thyme. Simmer gently, uncovered, for about 30 minutes to allow the flavors to meld.
2. Blend and Strain:
   - Remove the pot from heat and let it cool slightly. Remove and discard the bay leaf.
   - Use an immersion blender or transfer the mixture to a blender (in batches if necessary) and blend until smooth.
   - Strain the blended mixture through a fine-mesh sieve or cheesecloth into a clean pot, pressing down on solids to extract as much liquid as possible. Discard solids.

3. Finish the Bisque:
   - Return the strained liquid to the stove over medium heat. Stir in heavy cream and bring to a simmer.
   - Chop the reserved lobster meat into bite-sized pieces and add it to the bisque. Cook gently for 5-7 minutes, or until the lobster meat is heated through and tender.
   - Season the bisque with salt, freshly ground black pepper, and cayenne pepper (if using), adjusting to taste.
4. Serve:
   - Ladle the hot lobster bisque into bowls.
   - Garnish each serving with chopped fresh chives.
   - Serve immediately, accompanied by crusty bread or oyster crackers.

Lobster bisque is a decadent and flavorful soup that makes an impressive starter for a special meal. The rich, creamy texture and delicate seafood flavor make it a favorite among seafood lovers. Enjoy this homemade lobster bisque with loved ones for a restaurant-worthy dining experience at home.

Veal Saltimbocca

Ingredients:

- 4 veal cutlets (about 4-6 ounces each), pounded to about 1/4-inch thickness
- Salt and freshly ground black pepper
- 8 thin slices prosciutto
- 8 fresh sage leaves
- All-purpose flour, for dredging
- 4 tablespoons unsalted butter
- 1/2 cup dry white wine
- 1/2 cup chicken or veal broth
- 1 tablespoon fresh lemon juice
- 1 tablespoon capers, drained (optional)
- Chopped fresh parsley, for garnish

Instructions:

1. **Prepare the Veal Cutlets:**
   - Season both sides of each veal cutlet with salt and freshly ground black pepper.
   - Place 2 slices of prosciutto on each veal cutlet, covering them completely.
   - Place 2 sage leaves on top of the prosciutto on each cutlet, pressing them lightly to adhere.
2. **Dredge and Cook the Veal:**
   - Dredge each veal cutlet in flour, shaking off any excess.
   - In a large skillet, heat 2 tablespoons of butter over medium-high heat until melted and foamy.
   - Add the veal cutlets to the skillet, prosciutto-side down. Cook for 2-3 minutes until the prosciutto is crisp and lightly browned.
   - Flip the cutlets and cook on the other side for another 2-3 minutes until the veal is cooked through and golden brown. Transfer the cooked cutlets to a plate and tent with foil to keep warm.
3. **Make the Sauce:**
   - Deglaze the skillet with white wine, scraping up any browned bits from the bottom of the pan.
   - Add chicken or veal broth, lemon juice, and capers (if using). Bring the sauce to a simmer and cook for 3-4 minutes until slightly reduced.
   - Stir in the remaining 2 tablespoons of butter until melted and the sauce is smooth. Season with salt and pepper to taste.
4. **Serve:**
   - Arrange the veal saltimbocca on serving plates.
   - Spoon the sauce over the veal cutlets.
   - Garnish with chopped fresh parsley.
   - Serve immediately, accompanied by your favorite side dishes such as sautéed spinach, risotto, or roasted potatoes.

Veal Saltimbocca is a delicious and elegant dish that showcases the delicate flavors of veal, salty prosciutto, and aromatic sage. Enjoy this classic Italian favorite for a special dinner at home, paired with a glass of white wine for a complete dining experience.

Shrimp Scampi

Ingredients:

- 1 pound large shrimp, peeled and deveined
- Salt and freshly ground black pepper, to taste
- 4 tablespoons unsalted butter
- 4 tablespoons olive oil
- 4 cloves garlic, minced
- 1/2 cup white wine (such as Sauvignon Blanc or Pinot Grigio)
- 1/4 teaspoon red pepper flakes (optional)
- Zest of 1 lemon
- Juice of 1 lemon
- 1/4 cup chopped fresh parsley
- Cooked pasta or crusty bread, for serving

Instructions:

1. Prepare the Shrimp:
   - Pat the shrimp dry with paper towels and season with salt and freshly ground black pepper.
2. Cook the Shrimp:
   - In a large skillet, heat 2 tablespoons of butter and 2 tablespoons of olive oil over medium-high heat until the butter is melted and bubbly.
   - Add the minced garlic and cook for about 30 seconds until fragrant, stirring constantly to prevent burning.
   - Add the seasoned shrimp to the skillet in a single layer. Cook for 1-2 minutes per side, until the shrimp turn pink and opaque. Be careful not to overcook them. Remove the shrimp from the skillet and set aside.
3. Make the Sauce:
   - In the same skillet, add the white wine and red pepper flakes (if using). Bring to a simmer and cook for 2-3 minutes, scraping up any browned bits from the bottom of the skillet.
   - Stir in the remaining 2 tablespoons of butter until melted and the sauce starts to thicken slightly.
   - Add the lemon zest and lemon juice to the sauce. Stir to combine.
4. Combine and Serve:
   - Return the cooked shrimp to the skillet, tossing gently to coat them in the sauce.
   - Sprinkle chopped fresh parsley over the shrimp scampi.
   - Serve immediately over cooked pasta or with crusty bread for dipping, garnished with additional parsley if desired.

Shrimp scampi is a flavorful and satisfying dish that comes together in minutes. The combination of garlic, butter, white wine, and lemon creates a light and tangy sauce that perfectly complements the sweet flavor of the shrimp. Enjoy this classic seafood dish as a quick and delicious meal any day of the week!

Braised Short Ribs

Ingredients:

- 4 pounds beef short ribs, bone-in
- Salt and freshly ground black pepper, to taste
- 2 tablespoons vegetable oil
- 1 large onion, diced
- 2 carrots, diced
- 2 celery stalks, diced
- 4 garlic cloves, minced
- 2 tablespoons tomato paste
- 2 cups beef broth
- 1 cup red wine (such as Cabernet Sauvignon or Merlot)
- 2 bay leaves
- 2 sprigs fresh thyme (or 1 teaspoon dried thyme)
- Chopped fresh parsley, for garnish (optional)

Instructions:

1. Preheat the Oven:
    - Preheat your oven to 325°F (160°C).
2. Prepare the Short Ribs:
    - Season the beef short ribs generously with salt and freshly ground black pepper.
3. Sear the Short Ribs:
    - In a large Dutch oven or heavy-bottomed pot, heat the vegetable oil over medium-high heat.
    - Add the short ribs in batches, searing on all sides until browned, about 3-4 minutes per side. Transfer the seared short ribs to a plate and set aside.
4. Saute the Vegetables:
    - In the same pot, reduce the heat to medium. Add the diced onion, carrots, and celery. Cook for about 5-7 minutes, stirring occasionally, until the vegetables start to soften.
    - Add the minced garlic and tomato paste. Cook for another 1-2 minutes until the garlic is fragrant and the tomato paste darkens slightly.
5. Deglaze the Pot:
    - Pour in the red wine and scrape up any browned bits from the bottom of the pot with a wooden spoon or spatula.
6. Braise the Short Ribs:
    - Return the seared short ribs to the pot, along with any juices that have accumulated on the plate.
    - Add the beef broth, bay leaves, and fresh thyme sprigs (or dried thyme).
    - Bring the liquid to a simmer. Cover the pot with a lid.
7. Cook in the Oven:
    - Transfer the covered pot to the preheated oven.

- - Braise the short ribs for 2.5 to 3 hours, or until the meat is fork-tender and easily pulls away from the bone.
8. Serve:
    - Remove the pot from the oven. Discard the bay leaves and thyme sprigs.
    - Skim off any excess fat from the surface of the sauce, if desired.
    - Serve the braised short ribs hot, garnished with chopped fresh parsley if desired.

Braised short ribs are typically served with mashed potatoes, creamy polenta, or crusty bread to soak up the flavorful sauce. This dish is perfect for a cozy dinner at home, especially during cooler months when you crave hearty and comforting meals. Enjoy the tender, succulent meat and rich sauce of these braised short ribs!

Tuna Tartare

Ingredients:

- 8 ounces sushi-grade tuna, diced into small cubes
- 2 tablespoons soy sauce
- 1 tablespoon sesame oil
- 1 tablespoon fresh lime juice
- 1 teaspoon grated fresh ginger
- 1 teaspoon sriracha sauce (adjust to taste)
- 1 green onion, thinly sliced
- 1 avocado, diced
- 1 tablespoon sesame seeds, toasted (optional)
- Salt and freshly ground black pepper, to taste
- Fresh cilantro or microgreens, for garnish (optional)
- Wonton crisps or crackers, for serving

Instructions:

1. Prepare the Tuna:
    - Start with fresh sushi-grade tuna. Dice it into small, uniform cubes. Place the diced tuna in a mixing bowl.
2. Make the Dressing:
    - In a small bowl, whisk together the soy sauce, sesame oil, fresh lime juice, grated ginger, and sriracha sauce.
3. Combine Ingredients:
    - Pour the dressing over the diced tuna.
    - Add the thinly sliced green onion and diced avocado to the bowl with the tuna.
4. Season and Mix:
    - Gently toss all the ingredients together until well combined.
    - Season with salt and freshly ground black pepper to taste.
5. Chill:
    - Cover the bowl with plastic wrap and refrigerate the tuna tartare for at least 15-20 minutes to allow the flavors to meld together.
6. Serve:
    - When ready to serve, divide the tuna tartare among serving dishes or onto a platter.
    - Sprinkle toasted sesame seeds over the top for added texture and flavor (optional).
    - Garnish with fresh cilantro or microgreens, if desired.
    - Serve with wonton crisps, crackers, or crispy lettuce leaves for scooping.

Tuna tartare is a fresh and vibrant appetizer or light meal that showcases the delicate flavor of raw tuna, enhanced by the tangy, spicy dressing and creamy avocado. It's perfect for entertaining or as a special treat for yourself at home. Enjoy this elegant dish with friends and family!

Caprese Salad with Burrata

Ingredients:

- 8 ounces burrata cheese
- 2 large tomatoes, sliced (use ripe, flavorful tomatoes like Roma or heirloom)
- Fresh basil leaves
- Extra virgin olive oil, for drizzling
- Balsamic glaze or balsamic vinegar reduction, for drizzling (optional)
- Salt and freshly ground black pepper, to taste

Instructions:

1. Prepare the Ingredients:
     - Slice the tomatoes into rounds, about 1/4 inch thick.
     - Arrange the tomato slices on a serving platter or individual plates.
2. Assemble the Salad:
     - Tear the burrata cheese into smaller pieces and arrange them on and around the tomato slices.
     - Scatter fresh basil leaves over the tomatoes and burrata.
3. Season and Garnish:
     - Drizzle extra virgin olive oil over the salad, ensuring it covers the tomatoes and burrata.
     - Season with salt and freshly ground black pepper to taste.
4. Optional Drizzle:
     - For extra flavor, drizzle balsamic glaze or a balsamic vinegar reduction over the salad. This adds a sweet and tangy note to the dish.
5. Serve:
     - Serve the Caprese salad with burrata immediately, as a starter or side dish.
     - Enjoy the creamy texture of the burrata cheese with the juicy tomatoes and aromatic basil.

Caprese salad with burrata is a refreshing and simple dish that celebrates the flavors of summer. It's perfect for a light lunch, appetizer, or as part of a larger meal. Serve it alongside crusty bread or as a side to grilled meats or seafood for a complete and satisfying meal.

Peking Duck with Pancakes

Ingredients:

For the Duck:

- 1 whole duck (about 5-6 pounds)
- 1 tablespoon salt
- 2 tablespoons honey or maltose (for glazing)

For the Pancakes:

- 1 cup all-purpose flour
- 1/2 cup boiling water
- 1 tablespoon sesame oil
- Extra flour for dusting

For Serving:

- Hoisin sauce
- Thinly sliced cucumbers
- Thinly sliced scallions (green parts only)
- Thinly sliced carrots or radishes (optional)

Instructions:

Preparing the Duck:

1. Preheat the oven: Preheat your oven to 350°F (175°C).
2. Prep the duck: Rinse the duck under cold water and pat dry with paper towels. Trim off any excess fat.
3. Season the duck: Rub salt evenly over the duck, both inside and outside.
4. Glaze the duck: Brush the honey or maltose evenly over the duck skin.
5. Roast the duck: Place the duck breast side up on a rack in a roasting pan. Roast for about 2 to 2.5 hours, or until the skin is crispy and golden brown and the internal temperature reaches 165°F (74°C).
6. Rest and carve: Remove the duck from the oven and let it rest for 10-15 minutes before carving. Carve the duck into thin slices, ensuring each slice has a bit of crispy skin.

Making the Pancakes:

1. Prepare the dough: In a mixing bowl, gradually add boiling water to the flour while stirring with chopsticks or a wooden spoon until a dough forms.
2. Knead the dough: Transfer the dough to a lightly floured surface and knead until smooth, about 5 minutes. Cover with a damp cloth and let it rest for 30 minutes.

3. Shape the pancakes: Roll the dough into a long cylinder and cut into 12 equal pieces. Roll each piece into a ball and flatten with your palm. Brush each pancake lightly with sesame oil and dust with flour.
4. Cook the pancakes: Heat a non-stick skillet or griddle over medium-high heat. Cook each pancake for about 1-2 minutes on each side, until lightly golden and slightly puffed. Stack cooked pancakes and keep covered with a clean cloth to keep warm and moist.

Assembling the Peking Duck Pancakes:

1. Serve: To serve, spread a thin layer of hoisin sauce on each pancake. Add a few slices of roasted duck, thinly sliced cucumbers, scallions, and any optional vegetables.
2. Roll: Roll up the pancake and enjoy immediately.

Tips:

- You can find hoisin sauce, which is a sweet and savory sauce, in the international or Asian section of most grocery stores.
- To make the slicing easier, you can partially freeze the duck for about 20-30 minutes before carving.

Enjoy your homemade Peking duck pancakes as a delightful and flavorful meal that captures the essence of traditional Chinese cuisine!

Stuffed Lobster Tails

Ingredients:

- 4 lobster tails (6-8 ounces each), thawed if frozen
- 4 tablespoons unsalted butter, divided
- 1/2 cup breadcrumbs (preferably Panko)
- 2 cloves garlic, minced
- 1/4 cup grated Parmesan cheese
- 1/4 cup chopped fresh parsley
- Salt and freshly ground black pepper, to taste
- Lemon wedges, for serving
- Additional melted butter for brushing

Instructions:

1. Prepare the Lobster Tails:
    - Preheat your oven to 375°F (190°C).
    - Using kitchen shears, carefully cut through the top shell of the lobster tails lengthwise, stopping at the tail. Do not cut all the way through the tail.
2. Prepare the Stuffing:
    - In a small skillet, melt 2 tablespoons of butter over medium heat.
    - Add minced garlic and sauté for 1-2 minutes until fragrant.
    - Stir in breadcrumbs and cook, stirring frequently, until golden brown, about 3-4 minutes.
    - Remove from heat and let the breadcrumb mixture cool slightly.
    - Stir in grated Parmesan cheese, chopped parsley, and season with salt and pepper to taste.
3. Stuff the Lobster Tails:
    - Gently pry open the lobster tails and lift the meat slightly to rest on top of the shell.
    - Spoon the breadcrumb mixture evenly into the cavity of each lobster tail, pressing gently to pack it in.
4. Bake the Lobster Tails:
    - Place the stuffed lobster tails on a baking sheet or in a baking dish.
    - Melt the remaining 2 tablespoons of butter and drizzle over the stuffed lobster tails.
    - Bake in the preheated oven for 15-18 minutes, or until the lobster meat is opaque and the stuffing is golden brown and crispy.
5. Serve:
    - Remove the stuffed lobster tails from the oven.
    - Brush with additional melted butter if desired.
    - Serve hot with lemon wedges on the side.

Stuffed lobster tails are a luxurious dish that pairs well with a side of rice pilaf, roasted vegetables, or a fresh green salad. Enjoy this impressive seafood dish for a memorable meal at home!

Sushi and Sashimi Platter

Ingredients:

For Sushi Rice:

- 1 1/2 cups sushi rice
- 2 cups water
- 1/4 cup rice vinegar
- 2 tablespoons sugar
- 1 teaspoon salt

For Sushi and Sashimi:

- Assorted sushi-grade fish and seafood (e.g., tuna, salmon, yellowtail, shrimp, scallops)
- Nori (seaweed sheets)
- Vegetables (e.g., cucumber, avocado, radish)
- Pickled ginger
- Wasabi paste
- Soy sauce (for dipping)

Instructions:

1. Prepare the Sushi Rice:

   1. Rinse the sushi rice under cold water until the water runs clear to remove excess starch.
   2. Combine the rinsed rice and water in a rice cooker or pot. Cook according to the rice cooker's instructions or bring to a boil, then reduce heat to low, cover, and simmer for 15-20 minutes until the rice is tender and water is absorbed.
   3. In a small saucepan, heat the rice vinegar, sugar, and salt over low heat until dissolved. Remove from heat.
   4. Transfer the cooked rice to a large bowl or a wooden hangiri (sushi rice mixing bowl). Gradually add the seasoned vinegar mixture to the rice while gently folding and mixing with a rice paddle or wooden spoon. Be careful not to smash the rice grains. Let the rice cool to room temperature.

2. Prepare the Sushi and Sashimi:

   1. Slice the sushi-grade fish and seafood into thin slices for sashimi. For sushi, slice into strips or small pieces that fit onto nori sheets or atop rice.
   2. Cut vegetables into thin strips or julienne for sushi fillings.
   3. Prepare a bowl of water with a splash of rice vinegar to moisten your hands while handling the sushi rice to prevent sticking.

3. Assemble the Sushi and Sashimi Platter:

1. Arrange a variety of sushi and sashimi on a large serving platter or wooden sushi board. Place slices of sashimi neatly in rows.
2. Create sushi rolls by placing a sheet of nori on a bamboo sushi mat (makisu). Spread a thin layer of sushi rice evenly over the nori, leaving a 1-inch border at the top edge. Arrange fish, vegetables, or other fillings in the center of the rice.
3. Roll the sushi tightly using the bamboo mat, applying gentle pressure to shape the roll. Wet the top edge of the nori with water to seal the roll.
4. Use a sharp knife to slice the sushi roll into bite-sized pieces. Arrange the sushi rolls alongside the sashimi on the platter.
5. Garnish the platter with pickled ginger, wasabi paste, and small dishes of soy sauce for dipping.

4. Serve and Enjoy:

1. Serve the sushi and sashimi platter immediately, accompanied by extra soy sauce, wasabi, and pickled ginger on the side.
2. Encourage guests to enjoy the sushi and sashimi with chopsticks or their fingers, dipping each piece lightly into soy sauce and adding a touch of wasabi or pickled ginger as desired.

Tips:

- Freshness: Use only sushi-grade fish and seafood, which is safe to eat raw and has been properly handled and stored.
- Presentation: Arrange the sushi and sashimi neatly on the platter for an attractive presentation. Consider adding edible flowers, microgreens, or thinly sliced vegetables as decorative garnishes.
- Variety: Offer a variety of flavors and textures by including different types of fish, seafood, and fillings in your sushi and sashimi selection.

Creating a sushi and sashimi platter at home allows you to customize the selection to your preferences and showcase the beauty and freshness of these Japanese delicacies. It's perfect for special occasions or as an impressive appetizer for guests!

Pate en Croute

Ingredients:

For the Pâté:

- 1 lb (450g) pork shoulder, coarsely ground
- 1/2 lb (225g) pork liver, finely chopped
- 1/2 lb (225g) pork fatback, finely chopped
- 1 small onion, finely chopped
- 2 cloves garlic, minced
- 1 tablespoon brandy or cognac
- 1 teaspoon salt
- 1/2 teaspoon ground black pepper
- 1/4 teaspoon ground nutmeg
- 1/4 teaspoon ground cloves
- 1/4 teaspoon ground allspice
- 1/4 teaspoon ground ginger
- 1/4 teaspoon dried thyme
- 1/4 teaspoon dried sage
- 1/4 cup chopped fresh parsley
- 2 eggs (1 for the filling, 1 for egg wash)

For the Pastry Dough:

- 2 sheets of store-bought puff pastry dough (about 9x9 inches each)
- Flour (for dusting)

For Assembling:

- 2 slices of bacon, optional (for lining the mold)
- Dijon mustard (for brushing)
- 1 egg (for egg wash)

Instructions:

1. Prepare the Pâté Filling:

   1. In a large mixing bowl, combine the ground pork shoulder, chopped pork liver, and chopped pork fatback.
   2. Add finely chopped onion, minced garlic, brandy or cognac, salt, black pepper, nutmeg, cloves, allspice, ginger, thyme, sage, and chopped parsley. Mix well until thoroughly combined.
   3. Lightly beat 1 egg and add it to the mixture, mixing until evenly incorporated.

2. Prepare the Pastry and Mold:

   1. Preheat your oven to 350°F (175°C).
   2. If using bacon, line the inside of a pâté mold or a loaf pan with slices of bacon, leaving the ends hanging over the edges.
   3. Roll out one sheet of puff pastry dough on a lightly floured surface to fit the bottom and sides of the mold or loaf pan. Leave some overhang for sealing.

3. Assemble the Pâté en Croûte:

   1. Fill the pastry-lined mold with the pâté mixture, pressing it down firmly and leveling the top.
   2. Brush the top of the pâté mixture with Dijon mustard.
   3. Roll out the second sheet of puff pastry dough to cover the top of the mold. Place it over the pâté mixture and press the edges to seal with the bottom pastry, trimming any excess.
   4. Fold the overhanging bacon slices over the pastry if using, then fold the edges of the pastry over the top to create a neat seal. Crimp the edges with a fork or your fingers to seal completely.
   5. Beat the remaining egg and brush it over the top of the pastry to create a golden glaze.

4. Bake the Pâté en Croûte:

   1. Place the assembled pâté en croûte on a baking sheet lined with parchment paper.
   2. Bake in the preheated oven for 1 to 1.5 hours, or until the pastry is golden brown and crisp and the internal temperature reaches at least 160°F (70°C).
   3. Remove from the oven and let cool slightly before slicing.

5. Serve:

   1. Once cooled slightly, carefully remove the pâté en croûte from the mold or loaf pan and transfer it to a serving platter.
   2. Slice and serve warm or at room temperature, accompanied by cornichons, Dijon mustard, and crusty bread.

Pâté en Croûte is a labor of love that rewards you with a rich and flavorful dish perfect for special occasions or elegant gatherings. Enjoy this traditional French delicacy with friends and family!

Beef Carpaccio

Ingredients:

- 8 ounces beef tenderloin or sirloin steak, very thinly sliced
- 1 tablespoon extra virgin olive oil
- 1 tablespoon freshly squeezed lemon juice
- 1 tablespoon capers, drained and chopped (optional)
- 1/4 cup shaved Parmesan cheese
- Freshly ground black pepper, to taste
- Sea salt, to taste
- Fresh arugula or mixed greens, for serving (optional)
- Crusty bread or crostini, for serving

Instructions:

1. Prepare the Beef:
    - Ensure the beef is very cold before slicing. Place it in the freezer for about 15-20 minutes to firm up.
    - Use a very sharp knife to slice the beef as thinly as possible. Arrange the slices on a chilled serving platter in a single layer.
2. Make the Dressing:
    - In a small bowl, whisk together the extra virgin olive oil and freshly squeezed lemon juice. Season with salt and pepper to taste.
3. Assemble the Carpaccio:
    - Drizzle the dressing evenly over the sliced beef.
    - Sprinkle chopped capers (if using) and shaved Parmesan cheese over the beef slices.
4. Season and Serve:
    - Season with a little more freshly ground black pepper and a sprinkle of sea salt, if desired.
    - Serve immediately with fresh arugula or mixed greens on the side, and crusty bread or crostini.
5. Enjoy:
    - Beef carpaccio is best enjoyed right after assembling to preserve its freshness and delicate flavors.
    - Serve as an elegant appetizer or part of a light meal.

Tips:

- Quality matters: Use the best quality beef you can find, preferably from a trusted butcher.
- Thin slicing: For the best results, aim to slice the beef as thinly and evenly as possible. A sharp knife and slightly frozen beef make this easier.
- Customize: Feel free to adjust the dressing to your taste preferences, adding more lemon juice or olive oil as needed.

Beef carpaccio is a sophisticated dish that highlights the natural flavors of the beef, complemented by the tangy dressing and sharp Parmesan cheese. It's perfect for special occasions or when you want to impress with a simple yet elegant appetizer. Enjoy!

Chicken Satay with Peanut Sauce

Ingredients:

For the Chicken Satay:

- 1 lb (450g) chicken breast or thigh meat, cut into thin strips or cubes
- Bamboo skewers, soaked in water for 30 minutes (if using wooden skewers)
- 2 tablespoons vegetable oil
- 1 tablespoon soy sauce
- 1 tablespoon fish sauce
- 1 tablespoon brown sugar
- 1 teaspoon ground turmeric
- 1 teaspoon ground coriander
- 1 teaspoon ground cumin
- 1 clove garlic, minced
- 1 tablespoon lemongrass, minced (optional)
- Salt and pepper, to taste

For the Peanut Sauce:

- 1/2 cup creamy peanut butter
- 1/4 cup coconut milk (or more for desired consistency)
- 2 tablespoons soy sauce
- 1 tablespoon brown sugar
- 1 tablespoon lime juice
- 1 clove garlic, minced
- 1 teaspoon grated fresh ginger
- 1/2 teaspoon ground cumin
- 1/4 teaspoon cayenne pepper (optional, for heat)
- Water, as needed to adjust consistency

For Garnish (optional):

- Chopped peanuts
- Fresh cilantro or parsley
- Lime wedges

Instructions:

1. Marinate the Chicken:

    1. In a bowl, combine vegetable oil, soy sauce, fish sauce, brown sugar, ground turmeric, ground coriander, ground cumin, minced garlic, minced lemongrass (if using), salt, and pepper. Mix well.

2. Add the chicken strips or cubes to the marinade, ensuring they are evenly coated. Cover and refrigerate for at least 30 minutes, or up to 2 hours for more flavor.

2. Make the Peanut Sauce:

   1. In a small saucepan over low heat, combine creamy peanut butter, coconut milk, soy sauce, brown sugar, lime juice, minced garlic, grated ginger, ground cumin, and cayenne pepper (if using).
   2. Stir continuously until the mixture is smooth and heated through. If the sauce is too thick, add water gradually until it reaches your desired consistency. Remove from heat and set aside.

3. Prepare the Chicken Satay:

   1. Preheat your grill or grill pan over medium-high heat.
   2. Thread the marinated chicken onto the soaked skewers, leaving space between each piece.
   3. Grill the chicken skewers for 3-4 minutes on each side, or until cooked through and slightly charred. Cooking time may vary depending on the thickness of the chicken pieces.
   4. Remove from the grill and let the chicken satay rest for a few minutes.

4. Serve:

   1. Arrange the chicken satay skewers on a serving platter.
   2. Drizzle the peanut sauce over the chicken satay or serve it on the side for dipping.
   3. Garnish with chopped peanuts, fresh cilantro or parsley, and lime wedges if desired.

5. Enjoy:

   - Chicken satay with peanut sauce is best served warm. Enjoy it as an appetizer or main dish, accompanied by steamed rice or a fresh salad.

This recipe for chicken satay with peanut sauce brings together tender grilled chicken with a rich, flavorful peanut sauce that has a perfect balance of sweet, savory, and spicy notes. It's sure to be a hit at any gathering or as a special treat for yourself!

Smoked Salmon Canapes

Ingredients:

- 1 French baguette or similar crusty bread, sliced into rounds
- 8 ounces (225g) smoked salmon, thinly sliced
- 1/2 cup cream cheese or crème fraîche
- 1 tablespoon fresh dill, chopped
- 1 tablespoon capers, drained
- 1 small red onion, thinly sliced (optional)
- Freshly ground black pepper
- Lemon wedges, for garnish

Instructions:

1. Prepare the Bread:

    1. Preheat your oven to 350°F (175°C).
    2. Arrange the bread slices on a baking sheet in a single layer. Toast them in the preheated oven for about 8-10 minutes, or until they are lightly golden and crisp. Remove from the oven and let them cool slightly.

2. Prepare the Toppings:

    1. In a small bowl, mix the cream cheese or crème fraîche with chopped fresh dill until well combined.
    2. Drain the capers and pat them dry with a paper towel.

3. Assemble the Canapés:

    1. Spread a thin layer of the cream cheese or crème fraîche mixture onto each toasted bread round.
    2. Top each bread round with a slice of smoked salmon.
    3. Garnish each canapé with a few capers, a slice of red onion (if using), and a sprinkle of freshly ground black pepper.
    4. Arrange the smoked salmon canapés on a serving platter.

4. Serve:

    - Serve the smoked salmon canapés immediately, garnished with lemon wedges on the side.

Tips

- Variations: You can add additional toppings such as a squeeze of lemon juice, fresh herbs like chives or parsley, or a dollop of horseradish cream for extra flavor.

- Presentation: To make the canapés more visually appealing, you can fold the slices of smoked salmon into small rolls before placing them on the bread rounds.

Smoked salmon canapés are a wonderful addition to any appetizer spread. They are not only easy to prepare but also elegant and flavorful, making them a favorite among guests. Enjoy making and serving these delicious bites at your next gathering!

Vegetarian Spring Rolls

Ingredients:

For the Spring Rolls:

- Rice paper wrappers (also known as spring roll wrappers)
- 1 cup vermicelli rice noodles, cooked according to package instructions and cooled
- 1 cup firm tofu or tempeh, thinly sliced or cut into strips (optional)
- 1 cup lettuce leaves, shredded
- 1 cup cucumber, julienned
- 1 cup carrot, julienned or grated
- 1/2 cup fresh mint leaves
- 1/2 cup fresh cilantro leaves
- 1/2 cup fresh Thai basil leaves (optional)
- 1/4 cup roasted peanuts, chopped (optional)

For the Dipping Sauce:

- 1/4 cup hoisin sauce
- 2 tablespoons peanut butter
- 2 tablespoons water
- 1 tablespoon soy sauce
- 1 tablespoon rice vinegar
- 1 clove garlic, minced
- Sriracha or chili garlic sauce, to taste (optional)

Instructions:

1. Prepare the Fillings:

    1. Cook the vermicelli rice noodles according to the package instructions. Drain, rinse with cold water, and set aside to cool.
    2. If using tofu or tempeh, heat a little oil in a skillet over medium heat. Cook the tofu or tempeh until golden and crispy on both sides. Remove from heat and let cool.
    3. Prepare all the vegetables and herbs: shred the lettuce, julienne the cucumber and carrot, and pick the leaves from the mint, cilantro, and Thai basil (if using).

2. Prepare the Dipping Sauce:

    1. In a small bowl, whisk together hoisin sauce, peanut butter, water, soy sauce, rice vinegar, minced garlic, and Sriracha or chili garlic sauce (if using). Adjust the seasoning to taste and set aside.

3. Assemble the Spring Rolls:

1. Fill a large shallow dish or pie plate with warm water. Dip one rice paper wrapper into the water for a few seconds until it becomes pliable but still slightly firm.
2. Carefully transfer the softened rice paper wrapper to a clean, dry surface.
3. Layer a small amount of each filling ingredient (vermicelli noodles, tofu or tempeh if using, lettuce, cucumber, carrot, mint, cilantro, and Thai basil) in the center of the wrapper, leaving space on the sides.
4. Fold the sides of the wrapper over the filling, then fold the bottom edge up and tightly roll everything into a cylinder, sealing the top edge. Repeat with the remaining wrappers and filling ingredients.

4. Serve:

1. Arrange the vegetarian spring rolls on a serving platter.
2. If desired, sprinkle chopped roasted peanuts on top for added texture and flavor.
3. Serve the spring rolls with the prepared dipping sauce on the side.

Tips:

- Work with one rice paper wrapper at a time to prevent them from sticking together.
- Don't overfill the spring rolls to ensure they roll up neatly.
- You can customize the fillings based on your preferences and what you have on hand. Other options include avocado slices, bell pepper strips, or bean sprouts.

Vegetarian spring rolls are best enjoyed fresh, soon after assembling. They make a healthy and colorful appetizer or light meal that's perfect for warm weather or any time you crave a refreshing snack!

Roasted Vegetable Terrine

Ingredients:

- Assorted vegetables of your choice, such as:
    - Zucchini, sliced lengthwise
    - Eggplant, sliced lengthwise
    - Bell peppers, roasted and peeled
    - Tomatoes, sliced
    - Red onions, sliced
    - Carrots, sliced lengthwise
    - Mushrooms, sliced
- Olive oil
- Salt and pepper
- Fresh herbs, such as thyme, rosemary, or basil
- Balsamic vinegar (optional)
- Vegetable broth or stock
- Goat cheese or feta cheese (optional, for layers)
- Parchment paper

Instructions:

1. Prepare the Vegetables:

    1. Preheat your oven to 400°F (200°C).
    2. Prepare the vegetables: slice them into uniform thickness for even cooking. If using bell peppers, roast them whole in the oven until the skin is blistered, then peel off the skin, remove seeds, and slice.
    3. Toss the vegetables with olive oil, salt, pepper, and any herbs or balsamic vinegar (if using) for extra flavor.
    4. Roast the vegetables on baking sheets lined with parchment paper until tender and slightly caramelized. Cooking times may vary depending on the type and thickness of the vegetables. Remove from the oven and let cool.

2. Assemble the Terrine:

    1. Line a terrine dish or loaf pan with parchment paper, leaving enough overhang to cover the top of the terrine.
    2. Begin layering the roasted vegetables in the dish, alternating colors and types to create a visually appealing pattern. Press down gently after each layer to compact the vegetables.
    3. If using cheese, crumble or slice it and layer it between the vegetable layers.
    4. Continue layering until the dish is filled, finishing with a layer of vegetables on top.

3. Bake the Terrine:

1. Preheat your oven to 350°F (175°C).
2. Fold the parchment paper overhang over the top of the terrine to cover it.
3. Place a weight (such as a brick wrapped in foil or another heavy oven-safe object) on top of the terrine to compress it slightly.
4. Bake the terrine in the preheated oven for about 30-40 minutes, or until heated through and the vegetables are tender. This helps the flavors meld together.

4. Serve:

1. Remove the terrine from the oven and let it cool slightly.
2. Carefully remove the weight and parchment paper.
3. Slice the terrine into portions and serve warm or at room temperature.
4. Garnish with fresh herbs and a drizzle of olive oil if desired.

Tips:

- You can experiment with different vegetable combinations and seasonings based on your preferences.
- The terrine can be made ahead of time and refrigerated. Serve it cold or reheat gently in the oven before serving.
- Serve the roasted vegetable terrine with a side salad, crusty bread, or as a side dish to complement a main course.

Roasted vegetable terrine is a versatile dish that showcases the natural flavors of vegetables and makes for an impressive presentation. Enjoy making and serving this delightful dish for your next meal!

Wild Mushroom Risotto

Ingredients:

- 1 cup Arborio rice
- 4 cups vegetable or chicken broth (approximately)
- 1/2 cup dry white wine (optional)
- 1 tablespoon olive oil
- 2 tablespoons unsalted butter
- 1 small onion, finely chopped
- 2 cloves garlic, minced
- 8 ounces mixed wild mushrooms (such as porcini, shiitake, cremini), cleaned and sliced
- 1/2 cup grated Parmesan cheese
- 2 tablespoons chopped fresh parsley
- Salt and freshly ground black pepper, to taste
- Truffle oil (optional, for finishing)

Instructions:

1. Prepare the Broth:

    1. Heat the vegetable or chicken broth in a saucepan and keep it warm over low heat.

2. Sauté the Mushrooms:

    1. In a large skillet or frying pan, heat the olive oil and 1 tablespoon of butter over medium heat.
    2. Add the chopped onion and cook until softened and translucent, about 3-4 minutes.
    3. Add the minced garlic and cook for another 1-2 minutes until fragrant.
    4. Add the sliced wild mushrooms to the pan and sauté until they are tender and any liquid released by the mushrooms has evaporated, about 8-10 minutes. Season with salt and pepper to taste. Set aside.

3. Cook the Risotto:

    1. In a separate large saucepan or pot, melt the remaining tablespoon of butter over medium heat.
    2. Add the Arborio rice and toast it for 1-2 minutes, stirring constantly until the rice grains are well coated and slightly translucent around the edges.
    3. If using, pour in the white wine and cook until it has been absorbed by the rice, stirring frequently.
    4. Begin adding the warm broth to the rice, one ladleful (about 1/2 cup) at a time, stirring continuously.
    5. Allow each addition of broth to be absorbed by the rice before adding the next ladleful. Stir frequently to prevent the rice from sticking to the bottom of the pan.

6. Continue this process until the rice is creamy and tender, but still slightly al dente, about 18-20 minutes. You may not need all of the broth.

4. Finish the Risotto:

   1. Once the rice is cooked to your desired consistency, stir in the sautéed mushrooms along with any accumulated juices.
   2. Add the grated Parmesan cheese and chopped parsley. Stir well to combine.
   3. Season with additional salt and pepper to taste, if needed.
   4. For an extra touch of luxury, drizzle with a small amount of truffle oil just before serving (optional).

5. Serve:

   1. Divide the wild mushroom risotto among serving bowls or plates.
   2. Garnish with additional grated Parmesan cheese and chopped parsley, if desired.
   3. Serve immediately while hot.

Tips:

- Use a combination of wild mushrooms for the best flavor. If fresh wild mushrooms are not available, you can use dried mushrooms that have been rehydrated in hot water.
- Stirring the risotto frequently helps release the starch from the rice, creating a creamy texture.
- Arborio rice is preferred for risotto due to its high starch content, which gives risotto its characteristic creaminess.

Wild mushroom risotto is a comforting and flavorful dish that makes a satisfying main course or a delicious side dish. Enjoy the earthy flavors and creamy texture of this classic Italian dish!

Greek Mezze Platter

Ingredients:

For the Mezze Platter:

- Hummus (store-bought or homemade)
- Tzatziki sauce (store-bought or homemade)
- Greek olives (such as Kalamata or green olives)
- Feta cheese, cubed or crumbled
- Dolmas (stuffed grape leaves)
- Cherry tomatoes
- Cucumber, sliced
- Red bell pepper, sliced
- Radishes, sliced
- Red onion, thinly sliced
- Fresh herbs, such as dill, parsley, or mint, for garnish
- Extra virgin olive oil, for drizzling
- Lemon wedges, for serving
- Pita bread or sliced baguette, for serving

For Hummus (optional):

- 1 can (15 oz) chickpeas, drained and rinsed
- 2-3 tablespoons tahini
- 2 cloves garlic, minced
- Juice of 1 lemon
- 2-3 tablespoons extra virgin olive oil
- Salt and pepper, to taste
- Water, as needed to adjust consistency

For Tzatziki Sauce (optional):

- 1 cup Greek yogurt
- 1/2 cucumber, grated and squeezed dry
- 1-2 cloves garlic, minced
- 1 tablespoon extra virgin olive oil
- 1 tablespoon lemon juice
- 1 tablespoon chopped fresh dill (or mint)
- Salt and pepper, to taste

Instructions:

1. Prepare the Hummus (if making from scratch):

1. In a food processor, combine chickpeas, tahini, minced garlic, lemon juice, and extra virgin olive oil. Process until smooth.
2. Gradually add water, 1 tablespoon at a time, until the hummus reaches your desired creamy consistency. Season with salt and pepper to taste.
3. Transfer the hummus to a serving bowl and drizzle with olive oil.

2. Prepare the Tzatziki Sauce (if making from scratch):

1. In a bowl, combine Greek yogurt, grated cucumber, minced garlic, extra virgin olive oil, lemon juice, chopped fresh dill (or mint), salt, and pepper. Mix well.
2. Adjust seasoning to taste. Transfer to a serving bowl and drizzle with a little extra virgin olive oil.

3. Assemble the Mezze Platter:

1. Arrange small bowls or plates on a large serving platter.
2. Place the hummus and tzatziki sauce in separate bowls on the platter.
3. Arrange the Greek olives, feta cheese, dolmas, cherry tomatoes, cucumber slices, red bell pepper slices, radish slices, and thinly sliced red onion around the bowls.
4. Garnish with fresh herbs such as dill, parsley, or mint.
5. Drizzle extra virgin olive oil over the feta cheese and vegetables.
6. Serve the mezze platter with lemon wedges and pita bread or sliced baguette on the side.

4. Serve and Enjoy:

- Invite guests to assemble their own bites by spreading hummus or tzatziki on pita bread or baguette slices and topping with various components from the mezze platter.
- Enjoy the vibrant flavors and textures of this Greek mezze platter as a light meal, appetizer, or part of a larger Mediterranean-inspired spread.

Tips:

- Customize the mezze platter with your favorite Greek-inspired ingredients such as grilled vegetables, marinated artichoke hearts, or tzatziki variations.
- The mezze platter can be prepared in advance and assembled just before serving for convenience.
- Adjust the quantities of ingredients based on the number of servings and personal preferences.

A Greek mezze platter is not only delicious but also offers a colorful and appetizing presentation that is sure to impress your guests. Enjoy the Mediterranean flavors and the communal dining experience!

Venison Medallions with Red Wine Sauce

Ingredients:

For the Venison Medallions:

- 4 venison medallions, about 4-6 oz each (you can also use other cuts like loin)
- Salt and freshly ground black pepper
- 2 tablespoons olive oil
- 2 tablespoons unsalted butter
- 2 cloves garlic, minced
- Fresh thyme sprigs

For the Red Wine Sauce:

- 1 cup red wine (such as Merlot or Cabernet Sauvignon)
- 1 cup beef or venison stock
- 1 shallot, finely chopped
- 2 cloves garlic, minced
- 1 tablespoon balsamic vinegar
- 1 tablespoon Worcestershire sauce
- 1 tablespoon Dijon mustard
- 2 tablespoons unsalted butter, chilled
- Salt and freshly ground black pepper, to taste

For Garnish (optional):

- Fresh thyme leaves
- Parsley, chopped

Instructions:

1. Prepare the Venison Medallions:

   1. Pat dry the venison medallions with paper towels. Season both sides generously with salt and freshly ground black pepper.
   2. In a large skillet or frying pan, heat the olive oil over medium-high heat until hot but not smoking.
   3. Add the venison medallions to the skillet and sear for about 2-3 minutes on each side, depending on the thickness of the meat, for medium-rare doneness. Adjust cooking time based on your preferred level of doneness. Add the butter and garlic to the pan during the last minute of cooking, along with a few sprigs of fresh thyme, basting the medallions with the butter.
   4. Remove the venison medallions from the skillet and let them rest on a plate tented with foil while you prepare the sauce.

2. Make the Red Wine Sauce:

   1. In the same skillet over medium heat, add the chopped shallot and cook until softened, about 2-3 minutes.
   2. Add the minced garlic and cook for another minute until fragrant.
   3. Pour in the red wine and bring to a simmer. Allow the wine to reduce by half, scraping up any browned bits from the bottom of the skillet.
   4. Add the beef or venison stock, balsamic vinegar, Worcestershire sauce, and Dijon mustard. Stir well and simmer for about 5-7 minutes, or until the sauce has thickened slightly.
   5. Reduce the heat to low and whisk in the chilled butter, one tablespoon at a time, until incorporated and the sauce is glossy. Season with salt and freshly ground black pepper to taste.

3. Serve:

   1. Arrange the venison medallions on serving plates or a platter.
   2. Spoon the red wine sauce over the medallions, ensuring each piece is generously coated.
   3. Garnish with fresh thyme leaves or chopped parsley, if desired.
   4. Serve the venison medallions with red wine sauce immediately while hot.

Tips:

- Venison cooks quickly, so be careful not to overcook it to maintain its tenderness.
- You can adjust the thickness of the sauce by simmering it for longer to reduce further or adding a slurry of cornstarch and water to thicken.
- Serve the venison medallions with sides such as mashed potatoes, roasted vegetables, or a green salad to complement the flavors of the dish.

Venison medallions with red wine sauce are a sophisticated dish that highlights the unique flavor of venison with a rich and savory sauce. Enjoy preparing and savoring this elegant meal!

Sea Bass en Papillote

Ingredients:

- 2 sea bass fillets, about 6-8 ounces each
- Salt and freshly ground black pepper
- 1 tablespoon olive oil
- 1 lemon, thinly sliced
- 1 small zucchini, thinly sliced
- 1 small yellow squash, thinly sliced
- 1 small red bell pepper, thinly sliced
- 1 small red onion, thinly sliced
- 2 cloves garlic, minced
- 2 tablespoons white wine (optional)
- Fresh herbs, such as thyme, parsley, or dill, for garnish
- Parchment paper

Instructions:

1. Preheat the Oven:

    1. Preheat your oven to 400°F (200°C).

2. Prepare the Parchment Paper:

    1. Cut two large pieces of parchment paper, each about 12x16 inches in size.
    2. Fold each piece of parchment paper in half to create a crease down the center. Open it back up.

3. Prepare the Vegetables:

    1. In a bowl, toss together the sliced zucchini, yellow squash, red bell pepper, red onion, and minced garlic. Season with salt and pepper.

4. Assemble the Papillotes:

    1. Place half of the vegetable mixture on one side of each parchment paper, slightly off-center from the crease.
    2. Drizzle each sea bass fillet with olive oil and season both sides with salt and pepper.
    3. Place a sea bass fillet on top of the vegetables on each parchment paper.
    4. Top each sea bass fillet with a few slices of lemon and a sprinkle of fresh herbs.
    5. If using, pour 1 tablespoon of white wine over each fillet.

5. Seal the Papillotes:

    1. Fold the other half of each parchment paper over the fish and vegetables.

2. Starting at one end, make small overlapping folds along the edges to seal the papillote completely. Twist the ends to secure.

6. Bake the Papillotes:

    1. Place the parchment packets on a baking sheet and transfer them to the preheated oven.
    2. Bake for about 15-18 minutes, depending on the thickness of the fish fillets, until the fish is cooked through and flakes easily with a fork.

7. Serve:

    1. Carefully open the parchment packets (watch out for steam).
    2. Transfer each sea bass fillet with vegetables onto serving plates.
    3. Garnish with additional fresh herbs if desired.
    4. Serve immediately, directly from the parchment paper packets, allowing each guest to enjoy the aroma as they open their individual pouches.

Tips:

- Ensure the parchment paper is well-sealed to trap steam and flavors inside.
- Experiment with different vegetables and seasonings based on your preferences.
- You can substitute sea bass with other fish such as cod, salmon, or halibut using the same cooking method.

Sea bass en papillote is a healthy and flavorful dish that's also visually impressive when served. Enjoy the tender fish and vegetables infused with aromatic herbs and lemon!

Baked Alaska

Ingredients:

For the Cake:

- 1 prepared cake layer (store-bought or homemade), about 8 inches in diameter and 1 inch thick (sponge cake or pound cake works well)

For the Ice Cream Layer:

- 1 pint (2 cups) ice cream of your choice, slightly softened (traditional flavors like vanilla, chocolate, or strawberry work best)

For the Meringue:

- 4 large egg whites, at room temperature
- 1/2 cup granulated sugar
- 1/4 teaspoon cream of tartar
- 1/2 teaspoon vanilla extract

Instructions:

1. Prepare the Cake and Ice Cream Layer:

   1. Line a 9-inch round cake pan with plastic wrap, leaving enough overhang to easily lift out the ice cream layer later.
   2. Place the prepared cake layer at the bottom of the cake pan.
   3. Spread the softened ice cream evenly over the cake layer, smoothing the top with a spatula. Make sure the ice cream layer is compact and even.
   4. Cover with plastic wrap and freeze for at least 2 hours, or until firm.

2. Assemble the Baked Alaska:

   1. Preheat your oven to 475°F (245°C) and position the rack in the upper third of the oven.
   2. Once the ice cream layer is firm, remove the cake pan from the freezer. Lift out the ice cream layer using the plastic wrap and place it on a baking sheet.
   3. Quickly cover the entire ice cream layer and cake with the meringue (see instructions below).

3. Make the Meringue:

   1. In a clean, dry mixing bowl, beat the egg whites with an electric mixer on medium speed until frothy.
   2. Add the cream of tartar and continue beating until soft peaks form.

3. Gradually add the sugar, a tablespoon at a time, while continuing to beat on high speed until stiff, glossy peaks form.
4. Beat in the vanilla extract until incorporated.

4. Cover with Meringue:

    1. Remove the plastic wrap from the ice cream and cake layer.
    2. Working quickly, spread the meringue evenly over the entire surface of the ice cream and cake, making sure to seal the edges completely with meringue to prevent any air from getting underneath.
    3. Use the back of a spoon or spatula to create decorative peaks in the meringue.

5. Bake the Baked Alaska:

    1. Place the baking sheet with the assembled Baked Alaska in the preheated oven.
    2. Bake for 3-5 minutes, or until the meringue is lightly golden brown and toasted. Watch carefully to avoid burning.
    3. Remove from the oven and serve immediately, or return to the freezer to firm up for a few minutes before serving.

6. Serve:

    1. Slice and serve the Baked Alaska immediately while the meringue is still warm and the ice cream is firm.
    2. Optionally, you can flambe the Baked Alaska with a small amount of alcohol (such as rum or brandy) for a dramatic presentation before serving.

Tips:

- Work quickly when assembling and covering the Baked Alaska with meringue to prevent the ice cream from melting.
- Make sure your oven is fully preheated and hot before baking to quickly brown the meringue without melting the ice cream.
- Leftover Baked Alaska can be stored in the freezer, tightly wrapped in plastic wrap, for a few days. However, the meringue may lose its texture upon refreezing.

Baked Alaska is a classic dessert that impresses with its combination of textures and flavors. Enjoy making and serving this delightful treat for special occasions!

Chocolate Fondue Fountain

Ingredients and Equipment:

- Chocolate (dark, milk, or white chocolate) suitable for melting
- Fresh fruits (such as strawberries, pineapple chunks, bananas)
- Marshmallows
- Pretzel sticks
- Cubes of pound cake or angel food cake
- Skewers or fondue forks
- Chocolate fondue fountain
- Optional: Nuts, cookies, dried fruits for dipping

Instructions:

1. Prepare the Chocolate:

    1. Choose your favorite chocolate (dark, milk, or white) and chop it into small pieces for quicker melting. You can also use chocolate chips or melting wafers designed for fondue fountains.
    2. Melt the chocolate using a microwave-safe bowl or a double boiler. If using a microwave, heat in short intervals (about 30 seconds each) and stir between each interval until smooth and melted. Be careful not to overheat the chocolate.
    3. Once melted, pour the chocolate into the base of the fondue fountain. Most fountains have a reservoir at the base where the melted chocolate is poured.

2. Set Up the Fondue Fountain:

    1. Assemble the chocolate fondue fountain according to the manufacturer's instructions. Ensure all parts are securely in place.
    2. Turn on the fountain and adjust the heat setting if your fountain has a heating element to keep the chocolate melted and flowing smoothly.

3. Prepare Dipping Items:

    1. Wash and prepare the fruits and other items for dipping. Cut larger fruits into bite-sized pieces, and skewer smaller items like marshmallows or pretzel sticks for easier dipping.
    2. Arrange the prepared dipping items on serving platters or trays around the chocolate fountain. Provide skewers or fondue forks for guests to use.

4. Enjoy the Chocolate Fountain:

    1. Invite guests to dip their chosen items into the flowing chocolate. Encourage them to hold the skewered items under the flowing chocolate to coat them thoroughly.

2. Use the provided skewers or fondue forks to lift the coated items out of the fountain and onto their plates.
3. Enjoy the chocolate-coated treats immediately while the chocolate is warm and smooth.

5. Maintain the Fountain:

1. Monitor the level of chocolate in the fountain throughout your event. Add more melted chocolate as needed to keep the fountain flowing smoothly.
2. Stir the chocolate occasionally to ensure even consistency and flow.

Tips:

- Choose high-quality chocolate for best results. Dark chocolate is often preferred for its rich flavor, but you can use milk or white chocolate according to your preference.
- Offer a variety of dipping items to cater to different tastes. Consider adding nuts, cookies, or dried fruits for a diverse selection.
- Place napkins or paper towels near the fountain to catch any drips or spills.

A chocolate fondue fountain is sure to be a hit at any party or gathering, providing a fun and delicious experience for guests of all ages. Enjoy the interactive and indulgent treat!

Macarons Assortment

Ingredients:

For the Macaron Shells:

- 100 grams aged egg whites (about 3 large eggs)
- 50 grams granulated sugar
- 200 grams powdered sugar
- 110 grams almond flour
- Gel food coloring (optional)
- Flavor extracts (optional, such as vanilla, almond, or citrus)

For the Filling:

- 150 grams unsalted butter, softened
- 200 grams powdered sugar
- Flavor extracts or jams (to taste)
- Food coloring (optional for tinting the filling)

Instructions:

1. Prepare the Macaron Shells:

   1. Prepare Baking Sheets: Line two baking sheets with parchment paper or silicone mats.
   2. Prepare Almond Mixture: In a food processor, combine almond flour and powdered sugar. Pulse until well combined and there are no lumps. Sieve the mixture into a large bowl.
   3. Make Meringue: In a clean, dry bowl, beat the egg whites on medium speed until foamy. Gradually add granulated sugar, a tablespoon at a time, while continuing to beat. Increase speed to high and beat until stiff peaks form. Add gel food coloring and flavor extracts if using.
   4. Macaronage: Gently fold the almond mixture into the meringue in three additions until the batter is smooth and shiny, with a lava-like consistency. Be careful not to overmix.
   5. Pipe Macarons: Transfer the batter into a piping bag fitted with a round tip. Pipe small rounds (about 1-1.5 inches in diameter) onto the prepared baking sheets, spacing them about 1 inch apart. Tap the baking sheets on the counter to release air bubbles.
   6. Rest and Preheat: Let the piped macarons sit at room temperature for 30-60 minutes until a skin forms on top (they should not stick to your finger when lightly touched). Meanwhile, preheat your oven to 300°F (150°C).
   7. Bake: Bake the macarons, one sheet at a time, for 15-18 minutes, rotating halfway through baking, until set and firm. Let cool completely on the baking sheet before removing.

2. Prepare the Filling:

1. **Cream Butter:** In a mixing bowl, beat the softened butter until creamy and smooth.
2. **Add Sugar:** Gradually add powdered sugar, beating until light and fluffy. Add flavor extracts or jams to taste and beat until well combined.
3. **Color and Flavor:** Add food coloring if desired to tint the filling. Adjust consistency with more powdered sugar or a splash of milk, if needed.

3. Assemble the Macarons:

1. **Match Pairs:** Match macaron shells of similar size and shape into pairs.
2. **Fill:** Transfer the filling to a piping bag fitted with a round tip. Pipe a dollop of filling onto the flat side of one shell, then gently sandwich with another shell.
3. **Age (Optional):** Place filled macarons in an airtight container and refrigerate for 24-48 hours. This aging process helps develop flavors and texture.
4. **Serve:** Bring macarons to room temperature before serving. Arrange them on a platter and enjoy your assortment of flavors!

Tips:

- **Aging Egg Whites:** Separate egg whites and let them age at room temperature for 24-48 hours, covered with a paper towel, to reduce moisture and achieve a better meringue.
- **Consistency:** The key to successful macarons is achieving the right consistency in both the meringue and the almond mixture. Practice folding gently until the batter flows smoothly off the spatula.
- **Storage:** Store filled macarons in an airtight container in the refrigerator for up to 5 days. Bring to room temperature before serving.

By following these steps, you can create a beautiful assortment of macarons with various flavors and colors to delight your guests or enjoy yourself!

Miniature Cheesecakes

Ingredients:

For the Crust:

- 1 cup graham cracker crumbs (about 8-10 full sheets)
- 3 tablespoons unsalted butter, melted
- 1 tablespoon granulated sugar

For the Cheesecake Filling:

- 2 packages (16 ounces total) cream cheese, softened
- 1/2 cup granulated sugar
- 2 large eggs, at room temperature
- 1 teaspoon vanilla extract
- 1/4 cup sour cream or Greek yogurt

Optional Toppings:

- Fresh berries, fruit compote, chocolate ganache, whipped cream, etc.

Instructions:

1. Preheat the Oven:

    1. Preheat your oven to 325°F (160°C). Line a muffin tin with paper liners or use silicone muffin cups for easy removal.

2. Prepare the Crust:

    1. In a bowl, combine the graham cracker crumbs, melted butter, and sugar. Mix until the crumbs are evenly moistened.
    2. Divide the mixture evenly among the muffin cups, about 1 tablespoon per cup.
    3. Press the crumbs firmly into the bottom of each cup using the back of a spoon or your fingers to form a compact crust.

3. Make the Cheesecake Filling:

    1. In a large mixing bowl, beat the softened cream cheese and sugar until smooth and creamy, about 2-3 minutes, scraping down the sides of the bowl as needed.
    2. Add the eggs one at a time, beating well after each addition until fully incorporated.
    3. Mix in the vanilla extract and sour cream (or Greek yogurt) until smooth and creamy.

4. Fill the Muffin Cups:

1. Spoon the cheesecake filling evenly over the crusts in the muffin tin, filling each cup almost to the top.
2. Smooth the tops of the cheesecakes with a spatula.

5. Bake the Mini Cheesecakes:

1. Place the muffin tin in the preheated oven and bake for 18-20 minutes, or until the edges are set and the centers are slightly jiggly.
2. Remove from the oven and let the cheesecakes cool in the muffin tin for 10 minutes.
3. Transfer the cheesecakes to a wire rack to cool completely, then refrigerate for at least 2 hours or overnight to set.

6. Serve and Garnish:

1. Once chilled and set, carefully remove the paper liners from the cheesecakes.
2. Serve the miniature cheesecakes plain or with your favorite toppings such as fresh berries, fruit compote, chocolate ganache, or whipped cream.

Tips:

- Ensure that the cream cheese is softened at room temperature to avoid lumps in the cheesecake batter.
- Avoid over-mixing the batter once the eggs are added to prevent incorporating too much air, which can lead to cracks in the cheesecakes.
- Refrigerate the cheesecakes for at least 2 hours before serving to allow them to firm up and develop flavors.

Miniature cheesecakes are perfect for parties, gatherings, or simply as a delicious treat for yourself. They are easy to portion and serve, making them a versatile dessert option for any occasion!

Raspberry White Chocolate Mousse

Ingredients:

- 1 cup fresh raspberries
- 1/4 cup granulated sugar (adjust to taste depending on sweetness of raspberries)
- 1 tablespoon lemon juice
- 1 teaspoon gelatin powder
- 2 tablespoons cold water
- 200 grams white chocolate, chopped (or white chocolate chips)
- 1 1/2 cups heavy cream, chilled
- Fresh raspberries and mint leaves, for garnish

Instructions:

1. Prepare the Raspberry Puree:

    1. In a blender or food processor, puree the fresh raspberries until smooth.
    2. Strain the raspberry puree through a fine-mesh sieve into a bowl to remove the seeds. You should have about 1/2 cup of raspberry puree.
    3. Stir in the granulated sugar and lemon juice into the raspberry puree. Taste and adjust sweetness if needed. Set aside.

2. Bloom the Gelatin:

    1. In a small bowl, sprinkle the gelatin powder over the cold water. Let it sit for about 5 minutes to bloom and soften.
    2. Microwave the gelatin mixture for about 10-15 seconds, until completely dissolved. Stir well and set aside to cool slightly.

3. Melt the White Chocolate:

    1. In a heatproof bowl set over a pot of simmering water (double boiler method), melt the chopped white chocolate, stirring occasionally until smooth and melted. Alternatively, melt in the microwave in short intervals, stirring between each interval until smooth.

4. Prepare the Mousse Base:

    1. In a mixing bowl, whip the chilled heavy cream until stiff peaks form.
    2. Gently fold the melted white chocolate into the whipped cream until well combined and smooth.
    3. Add the raspberry puree and gently fold it into the white chocolate whipped cream mixture until evenly distributed.
    4. Gradually add the dissolved gelatin mixture to the mousse mixture, folding gently to incorporate.

5. Chill and Serve:

    1. Divide the raspberry white chocolate mousse evenly among serving glasses or bowls.
    2. Cover with plastic wrap and refrigerate for at least 3-4 hours, or until set.

6. Garnish and Serve:

    1. Before serving, garnish each mousse with fresh raspberries and mint leaves.
    2. Enjoy chilled.

Tips:

- Use good quality white chocolate for best results, as it will contribute significantly to the flavor and texture of the mousse.
- Make sure the heavy cream is well chilled before whipping to achieve stiff peaks.
- Adjust the sweetness of the mousse by tasting the raspberry puree before adding sugar.

This raspberry white chocolate mousse is perfect for special occasions or elegant dinner parties. It's light, airy, and bursting with fruity and chocolatey flavors that are sure to impress your guests!

Strawberry Shortcake

Ingredients:

For the Shortcake:

- 2 cups all-purpose flour
- 1/4 cup granulated sugar
- 1 tablespoon baking powder
- 1/2 teaspoon salt
- 1/2 cup cold unsalted butter, cut into small pieces
- 3/4 cup cold heavy cream
- 1 teaspoon vanilla extract

For the Strawberries:

- 1 pound fresh strawberries, hulled and sliced
- 2-3 tablespoons granulated sugar (adjust to taste)
- 1 tablespoon fresh lemon juice

For the Whipped Cream:

- 1 cup cold heavy cream
- 2 tablespoons powdered sugar
- 1/2 teaspoon vanilla extract

Instructions:

1. Prepare the Shortcake:

   1. Preheat your oven to 400°F (200°C). Line a baking sheet with parchment paper or lightly grease it.
   2. In a large bowl, whisk together the flour, sugar, baking powder, and salt.
   3. Cut in the cold butter using a pastry cutter or your fingertips until the mixture resembles coarse crumbs.
   4. In a small bowl, mix together the cold heavy cream and vanilla extract. Pour the cream mixture into the flour mixture and stir until just combined. The dough will be slightly sticky.
   5. Turn the dough out onto a lightly floured surface and gently knead it a few times until it comes together. Pat or roll the dough into a circle about 1 inch thick.
   6. Use a round biscuit cutter (about 3 inches in diameter) to cut out circles of dough. Place the dough circles onto the prepared baking sheet, spacing them about 2 inches apart.
   7. Bake for 15-18 minutes, or until the shortcakes are golden brown. Remove from the oven and transfer to a wire rack to cool completely.

2. Prepare the Strawberries:

    1. In a bowl, combine the sliced strawberries, granulated sugar (adjust to taste), and fresh lemon juice. Stir gently to coat the strawberries evenly in sugar. Let them sit at room temperature for about 15-20 minutes to allow the juices to release.

3. Make the Whipped Cream:

    1. In a chilled mixing bowl, whip the cold heavy cream until it starts to thicken.
    2. Add the powdered sugar and vanilla extract. Continue whipping until stiff peaks form.

4. Assemble the Strawberry Shortcakes:

    1. To serve, slice each cooled shortcake in half horizontally.
    2. Place a spoonful of macerated strawberries on the bottom half of each shortcake.
    3. Top with a dollop of whipped cream.
    4. Place the top half of the shortcake over the whipped cream.
    5. Garnish with additional strawberries and a dusting of powdered sugar, if desired.

5. Serve:

    1. Serve immediately and enjoy the deliciousness of homemade strawberry shortcake!

Tips:

- For a variation, you can add a splash of balsamic vinegar or a sprinkle of freshly ground black pepper to the strawberries for a more complex flavor.
- Make sure to handle the dough gently to keep the shortcakes tender and light.
- Leftover shortcakes can be stored in an airtight container at room temperature for up to 2 days. Store any leftover strawberries and whipped cream separately in the refrigerator.

This strawberry shortcake recipe is perfect for spring and summer gatherings, or anytime you want to enjoy a classic and delightful dessert with fresh strawberries!

Tiramisu

Ingredients:

- 1 1/2 cups strong brewed coffee or espresso, cooled to room temperature
- 1/4 cup coffee liqueur (optional)
- 3 large eggs, separated
- 1/2 cup granulated sugar
- 1 teaspoon vanilla extract
- 8 ounces mascarpone cheese, softened
- 1 cup heavy cream
- 24-30 ladyfinger cookies (savoiardi)
- Unsweetened cocoa powder, for dusting

Instructions:

1. Prepare the Coffee Mixture:

    1. Brew strong coffee or espresso and let it cool to room temperature. Stir in the coffee liqueur if using. Pour into a shallow dish or bowl.

2. Prepare the Mascarpone Filling:

    1. In a large mixing bowl, beat the egg yolks and granulated sugar together until pale and creamy. Mix in the vanilla extract.
    2. Add the softened mascarpone cheese to the egg yolk mixture and beat until smooth and well combined.
    3. In a separate bowl, whip the heavy cream until stiff peaks form.
    4. Gently fold the whipped cream into the mascarpone mixture until smooth and creamy.

3. Assemble the Tiramisu:

    1. Dip each ladyfinger into the coffee mixture for about 1-2 seconds per side, ensuring they are soaked but not overly soggy. Arrange a layer of soaked ladyfingers in the bottom of a 9x9 inch or similar-sized serving dish.
    2. Spread half of the mascarpone filling evenly over the layer of ladyfingers.
    3. Repeat with another layer of soaked ladyfingers and the remaining mascarpone filling.
    4. Cover the dish with plastic wrap and refrigerate for at least 4 hours, or preferably overnight, to allow the flavors to meld and the tiramisu to set.

4. Serve:

    1. Before serving, dust the top of the tiramisu generously with unsweetened cocoa powder using a fine-mesh sieve.
    2. Cut into squares or scoop out portions with a spoon.

3. Serve chilled and enjoy!

Tips:

- Egg Safety: If you have concerns about using raw eggs, you can use pasteurized eggs or egg substitute products. Alternatively, you can heat the egg yolks and sugar mixture over a double boiler until it reaches 160°F (71°C) while constantly whisking, then proceed with the recipe.
- Ladyfingers: Make sure to use dry, crisp ladyfingers (savoiardi) for the best texture. Soft ladyfingers will become too soggy when soaked in the coffee mixture.
- Flavor Variations: You can customize your tiramisu by adding a layer of chocolate shavings or using different liqueurs like rum or amaretto in place of coffee liqueur.

Tiramisu is a decadent and elegant dessert that's perfect for special occasions or any time you want to indulge in a taste of Italy's culinary heritage!

Lemon Sorbet

Ingredients:

- 1 cup granulated sugar
- 1 cup water
- 1 cup freshly squeezed lemon juice (about 5-6 lemons)
- Zest of 1-2 lemons (optional, for extra lemon flavor)

Instructions:

1. Prepare the Simple Syrup:

    1. In a small saucepan, combine the granulated sugar and water over medium heat.
    2. Stirring occasionally, heat the mixture until the sugar completely dissolves and the liquid becomes clear. This creates a simple syrup. Remove from heat and let it cool to room temperature.

2. Prepare the Lemon Mixture:

    1. While the simple syrup is cooling, zest and juice the lemons. You should have about 1 cup of freshly squeezed lemon juice.
    2. If using lemon zest for extra flavor, grate the zest of 1-2 lemons and set aside.

3. Combine and Chill:

    1. In a mixing bowl, combine the cooled simple syrup, freshly squeezed lemon juice, and lemon zest (if using). Stir well to combine.
    2. Cover the bowl with plastic wrap and refrigerate the mixture for at least 2 hours, or until thoroughly chilled. Chilling the mixture helps to enhance the flavors.

4. Churn the Sorbet:

    1. Pour the chilled lemon mixture into your ice cream maker.
    2. Churn according to the manufacturer's instructions until the sorbet reaches a slushy, frozen consistency. This usually takes about 20-25 minutes.

5. Freeze the Sorbet:

    1. Once churned, transfer the sorbet into an airtight container. Smooth the top with a spatula.
    2. Cover the container with a lid or plastic wrap, pressing it directly onto the surface of the sorbet to prevent ice crystals from forming.
    3. Freeze the sorbet for at least 4 hours, or until firm.

6. Serve and Enjoy:

1. Before serving, let the sorbet sit at room temperature for a few minutes to soften slightly for easier scooping.
2. Scoop the lemon sorbet into bowls or cones. Garnish with fresh mint leaves or lemon zest curls if desired.
3. Enjoy the refreshing and tangy flavor of homemade lemon sorbet!

Tips:

- Variations: You can customize your sorbet by adding other citrus fruits like lime or orange juice. Adjust the sugar amount according to the tartness of the fruit.
- Storage: Store any leftover sorbet in the freezer in an airtight container for up to 2 weeks. Allow it to soften slightly at room temperature before scooping.
- No Ice Cream Maker? If you don't have an ice cream maker, pour the chilled lemon mixture into a shallow dish and place it in the freezer. Every 30 minutes, stir the mixture with a fork to break up ice crystals until it reaches the desired consistency.

Homemade lemon sorbet is a delightful dessert that captures the bright and zesty flavors of fresh lemons. It's perfect for serving as a palate cleanser between courses or as a light and refreshing conclusion to a meal!

Gourmet Cupcakes

Ingredients:

For the Cupcakes:

- 1 1/2 cups all-purpose flour
- 1 1/2 teaspoons baking powder
- 1/4 teaspoon salt
- 1/2 cup unsalted butter, softened
- 1 cup granulated sugar
- 2 large eggs, at room temperature
- 1 teaspoon vanilla extract
- 1/2 cup whole milk, at room temperature

For Chocolate Cupcakes (optional variation):

- Substitute 1/2 cup of flour with 1/2 cup unsweetened cocoa powder

Instructions:

1. Preheat and Prepare:

    1. Preheat your oven to 350°F (175°C). Line a cupcake tin with paper liners.

2. Mix Dry Ingredients:

    1. In a medium bowl, whisk together the flour, baking powder, and salt. If making chocolate cupcakes, whisk in the cocoa powder with the dry ingredients.

3. Cream Butter and Sugar:

    1. In a large bowl, cream the softened butter and sugar together until light and fluffy, using a hand mixer or stand mixer.

4. Acd Eggs and Vanilla:

    1. Add the eggs one at a time, beating well after each addition. Mix in the vanilla extract.

5. Alternate Mixing:

    1. Gradually add the flour mixture to the butter mixture in three additions, alternating with the milk, starting and ending with the flour mixture. Mix until just combined after each addition. Do not overmix.

6. Fill Cupcake Liners:

1. Divide the batter evenly among the cupcake liners, filling each about 2/3 full.

7. Bake:

   1. Bake in the preheated oven for 18-20 minutes, or until a toothpick inserted into the center comes out clean.

8. Cool:

   1. Remove from the oven and let the cupcakes cool in the tin for 5 minutes before transferring them to a wire rack to cool completely.

Decorating Gourmet Cupcakes:

1. Buttercream Frosting:

   - Use a classic vanilla buttercream frosting or try flavored variations like chocolate, strawberry, or cream cheese.

2. Filling (Optional):

   - Inject cupcakes with fillings like lemon curd, chocolate ganache, or fruit preserves for added flavor.

3. Toppings and Garnishes:

   - Decorate with fresh berries, chocolate shavings, edible flowers, sprinkles, or crushed nuts for texture.

4. Fondant and Decorations:

   - Experiment with fondant to create intricate designs, shapes, or characters for themed cupcakes.

5. Drizzles and Sauces:

   - Add elegance with chocolate ganache drizzles, caramel sauce, or flavored syrups.

6. Gourmet Flavor Combinations:

   - Try combinations like mocha espresso, salted caramel, red velvet, or matcha green tea for unique flavors.

7. Presentation:

   - Display cupcakes on tiered stands or decorative platters for a stunning presentation at parties or events.

Tips for Success:

- Room Temperature Ingredients: Ensure eggs, butter, and milk are at room temperature for even mixing and a smooth batter.
- Consistency: Use an ice cream scoop for even distribution of batter into cupcake liners.
- Cooling: Allow cupcakes to cool completely before frosting to prevent melting and sliding of decorations.

Creating gourmet cupcakes allows for personalization and creativity, making them perfect for celebrations or simply indulging in a sweet treat. Enjoy experimenting with different flavors and decorations to create your own gourmet cupcake masterpieces!

Profiteroles with Vanilla Cream

Ingredients:

For the Choux Pastry:

- 1/2 cup water
- 1/2 cup whole milk
- 1/2 cup unsalted butter, cut into small pieces
- 1 tablespoon granulated sugar
- 1/4 teaspoon salt
- 1 cup all-purpose flour
- 4 large eggs, at room temperature

For the Vanilla Cream Filling:

- 1 cup whole milk
- 1/2 vanilla bean, split lengthwise and seeds scraped out (or 1 teaspoon vanilla extract)
- 3 large egg yolks
- 1/4 cup granulated sugar
- 2 tablespoons cornstarch
- 1 tablespoon unsalted butter
- Fresh berries or powdered sugar, for garnish (optional)

Instructions:

1. Make the Choux Pastry:

   1. Preheat your oven to 400°F (200°C). Line a baking sheet with parchment paper.
   2. In a medium saucepan, combine water, milk, butter, sugar, and salt. Bring to a boil over medium heat, stirring occasionally.
   3. Reduce the heat to low and add the flour all at once. Stir vigorously with a wooden spoon until the mixture forms a ball and pulls away from the sides of the pan, about 1-2 minutes. Remove from heat.
   4. Let the mixture cool for 5 minutes. Add the eggs one at a time, beating well after each addition until smooth and glossy.
   5. Transfer the choux pastry dough to a piping bag fitted with a large round tip (or use a spoon). Pipe mounds of dough onto the prepared baking sheet, about 1 1/2 inches in diameter and 1 inch apart.
   6. Bake in the preheated oven for 15 minutes, then reduce the oven temperature to 350°F (175°C) and bake for an additional 20-25 minutes, or until the profiteroles are golden brown and puffed. Remove from the oven and let cool completely on a wire rack.

2. Make the Vanilla Cream Filling:

1. In a medium saucepan, heat the milk with the vanilla bean seeds (or vanilla extract) over medium heat until just simmering. Remove from heat and let steep for 10-15 minutes to infuse the vanilla flavor.
2. In a separate bowl, whisk together the egg yolks, sugar, and cornstarch until pale and creamy.
3. Gradually pour the warm milk into the egg yolk mixture, whisking constantly to temper the eggs.
4. Return the mixture to the saucepan and cook over medium heat, stirring constantly with a whisk, until thickened and bubbling, about 2-3 minutes.
5. Remove from heat and stir in the butter until melted and incorporated.
6. Strain the custard through a fine-mesh sieve into a clean bowl to remove any lumps. Cover with plastic wrap, pressing it directly onto the surface of the custard to prevent a skin from forming. Chill in the refrigerator until completely cold, about 1-2 hours.

3. Assemble the Profiteroles:

1. Once the profiteroles are completely cooled, use a small knife or a piping bag fitted with a small tip to make a small hole in the bottom of each profiterole.
2. Fill each profiterole with the chilled vanilla cream filling using a piping bag or a spoon.
3. Arrange the filled profiteroles on a serving platter.

4. Garnish and Serve:

1. Dust the profiteroles with powdered sugar and garnish with fresh berries, if desired.
2. Serve immediately, or chill in the refrigerator until ready to serve.

Tips:

- For a shortcut, you can use whipped cream or a prepared vanilla pudding as the filling.
- Ensure the custard is completely chilled before filling the profiteroles to prevent them from becoming soggy.

Profiteroles with vanilla cream are a decadent and elegant dessert, perfect for impressing guests or enjoying as a special treat. The light pastry and creamy filling combination make them irresistible!

Crepes Suzette

Ingredients:

For the Crepes:

- 1 cup all-purpose flour
- 2 large eggs
- 1/2 cup whole milk
- 1/2 cup water
- 2 tablespoons unsalted butter, melted
- 2 tablespoons granulated sugar
- 1/4 teaspoon salt
- Butter or oil for cooking

For the Suzette Sauce:

- Zest of 2 oranges
- 1 cup freshly squeezed orange juice (about 3-4 oranges)
- 1/2 cup granulated sugar
- 1/4 cup unsalted butter
- 1/4 cup Grand Marnier or Cointreau (orange liqueur)
- 1/4 cup brandy or cognac (optional)
- Orange segments (for garnish, optional)

Instructions:

1. Prepare the Crepes:

   1. In a large mixing bowl, whisk together the flour, sugar, and salt.
   2. In another bowl, whisk the eggs, then add milk, water, and melted butter. Whisk until well combined.
   3. Gradually add the wet ingredients to the dry ingredients, whisking constantly until the batter is smooth and free of lumps.
   4. Let the batter rest for at least 30 minutes at room temperature (or up to overnight in the refrigerator).
   5. Heat a non-stick skillet or crepe pan over medium heat. Lightly grease the pan with butter or oil.
   6. Pour a small ladleful of batter into the hot pan, swirling to coat the bottom evenly. Cook for about 1-2 minutes, until the edges of the crepe start to lift and the bottom is lightly golden. Flip and cook for another 30 seconds to 1 minute. Transfer to a plate and repeat with the remaining batter. You should get about 10-12 crepes.

2. Prepare the Suzette Sauce:

1. In a large skillet or shallow pan, combine the orange zest, orange juice, and sugar over medium heat. Stir until the sugar dissolves.
2. Add the butter to the pan and stir until melted and incorporated into the sauce.
3. Carefully add the Grand Marnier (or Cointreau) and brandy (if using) to the pan. Be cautious as the alcohol may ignite briefly.
4. Allow the sauce to simmer for 3-5 minutes, stirring occasionally, until it thickens slightly and reduces by about half. Remove from heat.

3. Flambe the Crepes (Optional):

1. Fold each crepe into quarters and add them to the pan with the Suzette sauce, arranging them in a single layer.
2. If desired, carefully ignite the alcohol by tilting the pan slightly over the gas flame (or use a long match) to flambe. Be cautious and stand back while doing this.
3. Let the flames die down naturally. Gently spoon the sauce over the crepes to coat evenly.

4. Serve:

1. Transfer the crepes to serving plates or a platter.
2. Garnish with fresh orange segments and a drizzle of the Suzette sauce.
3. Serve immediately while warm.

Tips:

- Flambe Safety: If you're not comfortable with flambeing, you can skip this step. The flavor of the dish will still be delightful without it.
- Make-Ahead: You can prepare the crepes and the sauce ahead of time. Reheat the sauce gently before adding the crepes.
- Variation: Some recipes use lemon instead of orange for a different twist on the classic dish.

Crepes Suzette is a luxurious dessert that combines delicate crepes with a tangy and sweet orange sauce, making it perfect for a special occasion or elegant dinner party. Enjoy the spectacle of preparing and serving this iconic French dessert!

Chocolate Truffles

Ingredients:

- 8 ounces (about 1 1/3 cups) good quality dark chocolate, finely chopped
- 1/2 cup heavy cream
- 1 tablespoon unsalted butter, at room temperature
- 1/2 teaspoon vanilla extract
- Cocoa powder, powdered sugar, chopped nuts, or melted chocolate (for coating)

Optional Coatings:

- Cocoa powder
- Powdered sugar (confectioners' sugar)
- Finely chopped nuts (such as almonds, hazelnuts, or pistachios)
- Melted chocolate (dark, milk, or white)
- Shredded coconut
- Sprinkles or edible glitter

Instructions:

1. Prepare the Ganache:

    1. Place the finely chopped chocolate in a heatproof bowl.
    2. In a small saucepan, heat the heavy cream over medium heat until it just begins to boil.
    3. Immediately pour the hot cream over the chopped chocolate. Let it sit undisturbed for 1-2 minutes to allow the chocolate to soften.
    4. Gently stir the mixture with a spatula or whisk until the chocolate is completely melted and smooth.
    5. Add the butter and vanilla extract to the ganache. Stir until the butter is melted and fully incorporated.
    6. If the ganache appears too thin or shiny, let it sit at room temperature to cool and thicken slightly, stirring occasionally.

2. Chill the Ganache:

    1. Cover the bowl with plastic wrap, pressing it directly onto the surface of the ganache to prevent a skin from forming.
    2. Refrigerate the ganache until it is firm enough to scoop and roll into balls, about 1-2 hours.

3. Shape the Truffles:

    1. Line a baking sheet with parchment paper.

2. Using a spoon or a small scoop, portion out small amounts of the chilled ganache and roll them between your palms to form smooth balls. Work quickly to prevent the ganache from melting too much.
3. Place the rolled truffles onto the prepared baking sheet. If the ganache becomes too soft, return it to the refrigerator to firm up again before continuing.

4. Coat the Truffles:

   1. Prepare your desired coatings in separate shallow bowls or plates. Examples include cocoa powder, powdered sugar, chopped nuts, or melted chocolate.
   2. Roll each truffle in the coating of your choice until evenly coated. Gently shake off any excess coating.
   3. Place the coated truffles back onto the parchment-lined baking sheet.

5. Set and Serve:

   1. Once all the truffles are coated, refrigerate them for at least 30 minutes to set.
   2. Transfer the truffles to an airtight container and store in the refrigerator until ready to serve.
   3. Serve the chocolate truffles chilled or at room temperature. They can be stored in the refrigerator for up to 2 weeks.

Tips:

- Use good quality chocolate for the best flavor. Dark chocolate with a cocoa percentage of 60% or higher works well.
- Experiment with different coatings and decorations to customize your truffles.
- For added flavor, you can infuse the cream with spices (such as cinnamon or cardamom) or liquors (such as rum or brandy) before making the ganache.

Homemade chocolate truffles are a decadent treat and make wonderful gifts or party favors. Enjoy the rich, creamy texture and intense chocolate flavor of these indulgent delights!

Fruit Tartlets

Ingredients:

For the Tart Crust:

- 1 1/4 cups all-purpose flour
- 1/2 cup unsalted butter, cold and cut into cubes
- 1/4 cup granulated sugar
- 1/4 teaspoon salt
- 1 large egg yolk
- 1-2 tablespoons cold water, if needed

For the Filling:

- 1/2 cup pastry cream or vanilla custard (store-bought or homemade)
- Fresh fruits such as strawberries, blueberries, raspberries, kiwi, etc., washed and sliced as needed
- Apricot jam or fruit glaze for brushing (optional, for a glossy finish)

Instructions:

1. Prepare the Tart Crust:

    1. In a food processor, combine the flour, sugar, and salt. Pulse a few times to mix.
    2. Add the cold butter cubes to the flour mixture. Pulse until the mixture resembles coarse crumbs and the butter is pea-sized.
    3. Add the egg yolk and pulse again until the dough starts to come together. If the dough seems too dry, add cold water, 1 tablespoon at a time, and pulse until the dough forms a ball.
    4. Turn the dough out onto a lightly floured surface. Shape it into a disk, wrap it in plastic wrap, and refrigerate for at least 30 minutes.

2. Preheat and Prepare:

    1. Preheat your oven to 375°F (190°C). Grease a mini tart pan or mini muffin tin with butter or non-stick cooking spray.

3. Roll Out and Shape the Dough:

    1. On a lightly floured surface, roll out the chilled dough to about 1/8 inch thickness.
    2. Using a round cookie cutter or a glass slightly larger than your tartlet molds, cut out circles of dough.
    3. Gently press each circle of dough into the greased mini tart or muffin tin, ensuring the dough fits snugly against the sides and bottom. Trim any excess dough if necessary.

4. Prick the bottoms of the tart shells with a fork to prevent them from puffing up during baking.

4. Bake the Tart Shells:

   1. Place the tart pan in the preheated oven and bake for 12-15 minutes, or until the tart shells are lightly golden brown.
   2. Remove from the oven and let the tart shells cool completely in the pan on a wire rack.

5. Assemble the Fruit Tartlets:

   1. Once the tart shells are cool, carefully remove them from the pan and place them on a serving platter or plate.
   2. Fill each tart shell with pastry cream or vanilla custard, using a spoon or piping bag.
   3. Arrange fresh fruit slices on top of each tartlet in a decorative pattern. You can mix and match fruits for a colorful presentation.
   4. Optionally, warm apricot jam or fruit glaze in a small saucepan over low heat until melted. Brush a thin layer over the fruit to give them a glossy finish and help preserve their freshness.

6. Serve and Enjoy:

   1. Refrigerate the fruit tartlets until ready to serve.
   2. Serve chilled and enjoy these delightful mini fruit tartlets as a sweet and refreshing dessert!

Tips:

- Make-Ahead: You can prepare the tart shells and pastry cream ahead of time. Assemble the fruit tartlets shortly before serving to keep the shells crisp.
- Variations: Experiment with different fillings such as lemon curd or almond cream. You can also try different combinations of fruits based on seasonal availability.
- Decoration: Garnish with fresh mint leaves or a dusting of powdered sugar for an extra touch of elegance.

These mini fruit tartlets are perfect for parties, gatherings, or as a special treat any time. They showcase the natural sweetness of fresh fruits combined with a buttery crust and creamy filling, making them a delightful dessert option!